What Is The Difference
Between Right and Wrong?

by Josh McDowell & Bob Hostetler

In easy-to-read International English,
a 1,500 word vocabulary of basic English words.

Gospel Publishing Mission

P.O. Box 1065 ~ Hobe Sound, FL 33475
www.gospelpublishingmission.org
A ministry of *Hope International Missions*

For information about other International English books visit
our web site at:
www.gospelpublishingmission.org

Derived from: *Right from Wrong*: what you need to know to help youth
make right choices by Josh McDowell & Bob Hostetler.
Copyright © 1994 by Josh McDowell. Josh McDowell Ministry,
P.O. Box 131000, Dallas, TX 75313; www.josh.org.
Original published by W Publishing Group,
a Division of Thomas Nelson, Inc.,
P.O. Box 141000, Nashville, Tennessee, 37214
Joseph E. Taylor, *Editor-in-chief*
Ralph L. Woodworth, Ph.D, *Editor/Translator*
Proofreaders: Erma Woodworth, John Jones, Joanna Baker,
Juanita G. Taylor, Sena Theall and Kathy Wright.

COVER ART BY ROBERT SCOTT / CLEAR GRAPHICS
(859) 363-3955

WHAT IS THE DIFFERENCE BETWEEN RIGHT AND WRONG?
IN INTERNATIONAL ENGLISH

ISBN 1-933716-05-3

Contents

Chapter 1

A Generation in Crisis

It was 11:30 at night. Elizabeth Pena and Jennifer Ertman called to tell their mothers they were on their way home from a party at a friend's house. They never got there. Because it was so late, the girls took a shorter way home through a group of trees. There they saw a group of boys. When the boys saw them, one of them called, "Get them!" The girls' naked bodies were found four days later. They had been raped many times before being killed.

Six boys were charged with the deaths. They were all between fourteen and eighteen years old. When one of the boys heard that they were charged with killing the girls, he said, "Great! Now we are really important!"

Counting Points

Billy Shehan claimed the most points with sixty-six. Dana Belman was next with sixty-three. Were they playing ball? No, they were playing a game called sex. Billy and Dana were part of a group that called itself the Spur Posse. The Spurs had become famous when a news reporter learned that they compared the number of each boy's sexual victories.

One girl said that a Spur would not return her clothes until she had sex with other Spurs. An eleven-year-old girl said that she was sleeping at a friend's house when a boy came in through the window. She agreed to have sex with him because she was afraid.

The boys admitted that they were just using the girls. "It has nothing to do with love," one of the boys said. Mike Weber, another Spur, said, "If you had sex, you got a point. That is all."

Troubled Young People

Why do our young people act that way? As Rowland Nethaway wrote in a story for the Cox News Service: "There have always been wild young people. But they knew what was right and what was wrong. Many of today's young people do not seem to know right from wrong."

Every day all across America, a thousand unmarried girls become mothers. More than a thousand unmarried girls have abortions. More than four thousand young people get a serious disease through having sex. Five hundred young people begin using drugs and a thousand begin drinking beer. Thousands of young people are beaten by other young people. Nearly a hundred girls are raped. Six young people kill themselves.

These things are not limited to young people who are "problem" young people. One study shows that among girls who are high school honor students, one in five said she had been a victim of a sexual attack. One in three knew someone who had brought a weapon to school. One in three had thought about killing herself. Four out of five of these honor students admitted to cheating.

We think our young people are not like that. They may have their problems, but they are good young people. Yet even as we praise our young people, we have to wonder. Could our young people become less like us and more like the world?

Living on the Edge

Like most Christian parents, you fear you will not be able to pass your values on to your children. You fear the influence of the public schools. You fear the influence of other young people. You fear the influence of television and popular music. You wonder if the teaching of the home and the church will be enough to protect your young people from those other influences. There is good reason to fear.

10

In March 1993, forty-two Christian leaders of young people joined me in Dallas, Texas.

For two-and-a-half days we talked about young people. We wondered just how much the culture was influencing young people from Christian homes and churches. To find out, we decided to ask a large group of young people a series of questions. We asked The Barna Research Group to direct the study for us.

We questioned more than thirty-seven hundred young people from all across the United States and Canada. They came from thirteen different groups of Bible-believing churches. These young people were involved in many church programs. Most of them said they came from good families where their parents loved them. More than half of them said they were Christians. Two out of three said that they prayed every day. Most of them attended Sunday school and youth group every week.

Yet they admitted that they were often involved in things their parents did not approve. Many of them were involved sexually. Many were lying, cheating and stealing. Far too many could not tell right from wrong.

How can we pass our values on to our children? How can we keep our young people from being drawn into the way of thinking that is ruining lives all around us? The government says the answer is better schools. Teachers say the answer is more money. Some people say we need more police, more punishment, more prisons, more jobs or more social programs.

Many of those things are good, but they do not really deal with the problem. We will never find the answer to the problem until we understand what the real problem is.

Chapter 2
Truth Matters

A friend of mine once thought about buying the house next to his. He planned to fix it up and rent it to good people. He thought that would improve his area and make it safer for his family.

He asked a friend who had experience in building to examine the house with him. My friend was disappointed at the work the house needed, but he remained hopeful. Then they went down to the area under the house. There his friend pointed out big broken places in the foundation. "This place is falling down," he told him. Pointing up to the house, he said, "Nothing you fix up there will help because of what is wrong down here."

That house is a picture of the problems our families face. The problems go deep into the very foundation of what people in our country believe. To deal with the problems, we must first find what causes them.

An Issue of Truth

Today's young people are so different from their parents and grandparents. One of the biggest reasons for that is that people do not remember why some things are right and other things are wrong. It used to be that everyone agreed on what was right and what was wrong. Parents, teachers and other adults all taught the same thing. That agreement made it easy to say what was right and what was wrong at all ages and in all conditions of life.

That has changed. Now most people do not believe it is possible to know what truth is. For them, truth is only one person's opinion. Each person does whatever he thinks is right.

13

Young people today are told "if it feels good, do it." All about them sin is made to look good. They are taught to laugh at the Bible. The public schools say they offer "value-free" education. Teachers say, "We cannot tell you what is right and what is wrong. You must decide that for yourselves. We can only point out the choices you have."

It is not hard to see that such teaching is not value-free at all. It teaches relativism, the belief that what is true for you may not be true for me. Relativism says that we cannot know what truth is or what is right or what is wrong.

We should not be surprised that seven out of ten young people today say that there is no such thing as truth. That is true both with young people who do not attend church and with those who do. Most young people say, "The only things you can know for sure are the things you experience in your own life." For them a thing is right if you think it is right and it is wrong if you think it is wrong.

We agree that people have a right to their own opinions. But we must accept that some things are clearly right and some things are clearly wrong.

Our Young People Do Not Know What to Think About Truth
More than half of our church young people agree that there is such a thing as truth under some conditions. If the question is asked in a different way, though, they change their minds. For example, most of them will say that the Bible clearly teaches truth about some things. Then they say that people cannot really understand the meaning of truth.

Seven of the questions we asked the young people were about general rules of truth and how to put truth to work in their lives. The answers the young people gave clearly show that they do not accept what the Bible teaches in those areas. Only one in ten of the young people always agreed with the Bible.

14

It is clear that the foundation on which many parents, pastors and other leaders are building is breaking down. Most young people from the church no longer trust the Bible. They do not find the Bible helpful in dealing with the problems they face. Even when they seem to understand and accept the truth the Bible teaches, they do not seem to be sure of themselves.

Our young people are not sure about who has the right to say what truth is. They are not sure about what truths they must accept or why they must accept them. As a result they make their choices without the guidance of God's truth.

What Is Absolute Truth?

By "absolute truth" I mean truth that is true for all people, for all times and for all places.

There is truth that is not absolute truth. For example, I have set a time when my daughter should be home after a ballgame. If she is home by that time, she is right. If she is not home by that time, she is wrong. Is that an absolute truth? No. It is not true for all people, for all times and for all places. Other people's daughters do not have to obey the rule I made for my daughter. As my daughter gets older, she may be allowed to stay out later. If I take my daughter someplace and stay there with her, she does not need to even think about the time rule.

If our children are going to learn how to know right from wrong, they must know what truths are absolute and why they are absolute. They need to know who establishes that truth and why.

Why Is Truth Important?

You may ask, "Do you really believe that what my children think about truth will affect the way they live?" Yes! That is one thing we saw most clearly from the questions we asked the young people. When young people do not accept absolute truth, they are more likely to lie to their parents. They are more likely to cheat on an examination. They are much more likely to try

15

to hurt someone, get drunk or steal. They are much, much more likely to use illegal drugs or try to kill themselves.

If young people do not accept absolute truth, they are less likely to trust people. They are more likely to be disappointed or angry at life. How our young people think about truth has a strong effect on how they live. It affects the choices they make, the way they feel about life and the way they treat other people.

What does it mean?
> Standard: a rule or object established to compare and judge thoughts, actions, or objects

When you accept absolute truth, you accept that there is an objective standard to tell right from wrong. By "objective standard" I mean a rule or set of rules that exists outside of yourself. You did not make those rules and you cannot change them. You believe that those rules are universal. That is, they do not change from person to person or from place to place. You believe that those rules are constant--they do not change from day to day.

When you accept that objective standard for truth, you use it to help you decide what is right and what is wrong.

Why Our Young People Accept Untruth

Instead of accepting absolute truth, our young people are accepting untruths. Because they have accepted the false ideas of the world, they cannot see that untruth is false. They think the true is false and the false is true.

Many young people in the church today believe it is not wrong to lie to a parent if you have a good reason. They think it is all right to cheat on an examination to get a better grade. They think it is all right to steal if the other person has more than you do. But you say, "Can they not see how wrong they are or how much pain they cause?" No, most of them cannot.

16

They think that if they have a reason that satisfies them, then anything they want to do is all right. That way of thinking, though, leads them to believe wrong choices are right ones. They accept the false truth and think they are getting the real truth.

Sin is often made to look innocent and desirable. It says you can have what you want right now without waiting for it. That is why so many young people choose sin. However, right choices often ask us to wait until some future time. But a false truth is still false. Too many young people are suffering from the results of the choices they make because they believe things that are not true.

I received a letter from a Christian father. He said that he and his wife had always done their best to be good parents. They belonged to a good church and had always been proud of their children. But they had just learned something about their oldest daughter that hurt them deeply. The father described his daughter as a pretty girl though she had never had boyfriends until recently.

Her first boyfriend was a member of the ball team. Not long after she started seeing him she had sex with him. She went from one team member to another. Before long she had had sex with every member of the team. By the time the parents learned what their daughter was doing, it had been going on for months.

The parents sat down with their daughter and told her they knew what had been going on. They cried with her and then asked, "Why did you do this?" The only answer she could give was, "I just wanted to feel loved. It never lasted very long, and I always felt bad about it later. But at least for a few minutes I felt that someone loved me."

Our children do not want that kind of false truth. They want the real thing. Without really accepting absolute truth, however, our children will accept the false kind almost every time. When they fail to accept truth as an objective standard, the way they think about life is wrong. Then they will accept false truths and begin to make wrong choices.

There Is Hope

It is a terrible thing to have to raise our children among a sinful and foolish people. King David's words are still true, "If the base of the building is destroyed, what can those who are right with God do?" (Psalm 11:3). There are no easy answers to that question, but there is hope. It is not too late to repair the broken base. However, we must not think we can do that easily. We will have to look honestly at what we in the church have permitted. We may have to begin changing things with ourselves.

I cannot tell how to fix our sinful world. I cannot tell how to raise perfect children. We live in an imperfect world. Not one of us is a perfect parent, pastor or church leader. Even young people from the best families and the best churches make terrible choices. In the end our children will decide for themselves about truth.

There are no easy answers, but there are answers. In this book we will show you a way to explain why absolute truths are absolute. We will show a way to teach young people and children how to tell which truths are absolute. Then we will show how to use absolute truth to examine eight areas of living. As you study these, you will learn to use this method to examine many other areas of life.

In the chapters that follow, we will tell the stories of three families. We will tell how each of those families faced a crisis of truth. These are not real families, but the things they faced are things that many families have faced.

Chapter 3

A Great Change

Seventeen-year-old Philip Milford followed his parents into his grandfather's nursing-home room. The room was dark and smelled like medicine. What little light there was came through a dirty window and thick curtains.

Philip's mother went to the window and opened the curtains. Then she turned and spoke to the old man. "There now, Daddy, that is better." The man looked at his daughter, the pastor's wife. He saw that Sarah, his nine-year-old granddaughter, stood with her father at the door.

"Sarah and I have to do some things, Dad. We will be back later," Pastor James Milford said.

"Okay, Jimmy boy," the old man said with a smile.

Mrs. Milford talked with her father a few minutes. Then she asked him if Philip could ask him a few questions for a school project. When the old man agreed, Philip's mother said she would be back a little later.

Philip looked at his grandfather. He hardly knew the eighty-year-old man. But this visit was for his school work. He took a pen and paper out of his pocket and said, "I guess I should ask you when you were born first."

The man did not answer. Philip looked at the clock. Finally the man spoke. "I was born first in 1914," he said. "I was born a second time some years later."

Philip looked long at his grandfather before writing down his answer. Then he raised his head and asked, "What was it like back then?" Philip waited for his grandfather to speak, but he only looked at the wall. Philip felt like forgetting the whole thing.

Finally the man spoke. "The first thing I remember is my father cutting wood. We were poor in those days. It seemed like my father spent most evenings cutting wood to heat our house. When I got older, I cut wood with him."

"Did you have electricity?"

He smiled. "No, we used oil lamps for light for reading and for family games. That was before television, of course."

"What did you do for fun?"

"I just told you. We played games together. I can remember when we got our first radio, too. I must have been about ten or eleven. Oh, and we would go on picnics during the summer."

"Did you fight with your parents?"

The man looked at Philip for the first time. "No," he answered. "There were things I did not like. I did not like having to cut wood. But they were my parents, and I did what they said."

Philip stopped writing. He was thinking that his grandfather probably just did not remember what it was like to be young.

"Of course," the old man continued, "it was not that way with everyone. I remember when Viola Kenton got her hair cut short and started wearing short skirts. I remember my parents talking about poor Mrs. Kenton."

The door opened and Mrs. Milford looked into the room. "Are you almost done?"

20

"Yes," Philip said. "I think so." He stood up as his parents entered the room. "Thanks, Grandpa."

"Come back sometime," the old man said. "I will tell you how I had to walk two miles to school every morning and four miles to get home!"

"Sure, Grandpa," Philip said.

Learning from History

Our children live in a world very different from the world of their grandfathers. Fathers and sons used to cut wood together. Families read books together and played together. People depended on God and on one another. Today most children do not grow up to do the same kind of work as their parents did. Parents and children spend little time together.

This change did not happen all at once. Nor is our recent crisis of truth new. That crisis has grown out of how people look at God and the world. So before we discuss how to tell right from wrong, we must look at this change over hundreds of years. If we do not understand this change, we probably will not understand the size of the problem.

In fact, the change goes all the way back to the Garden of Eden. There Satan got our first parents to trust their own thinking instead of obeying God.

In the days of Samuel, the leaders of Israel came to Samuel and said, "Give us a king like all the other nations have." God had been their King for hundreds of years. Any time something wonderful happened, everyone agreed that it was God Who had done it for them.

God told Samuel, "They no longer want Me to be their King. Do what they say. Give them a man to be their king. But warn them of what their king will demand of them." Samuel obeyed, but the people rejected Samuel's warning and demanded their own way.

Why was it wrong for the people to want a king? Perhaps it was not so wrong to want a king to lead them in battle. It was wrong, though, to put a man in the place of God. Their mistake was in thinking that human leadership would be better than following God. God wanted His people to look to Him for guidance. He wanted them to depend on Him. He wanted to take care of them. He knew that even the best man among them could not take better care of them than He could. He knew that the change would rob His people of many blessings.

The Birth of Modern Culture

What has happened in the past several hundred years is like Israel's demand for a king. Our culture has decided that truth and the rules of right living come from man, not from God. We have put man in God's place.

For hundreds of years in the West, everyone agreed with what the Bible teaches about what God is like. They agreed that truth and the rules for right living come from the nature of God. People were sure that the Bible was true in an absolute sense. That gave them a good way to discuss questions about right and wrong.

That all began to change during the period of European history we now call the Renaissance. The Renaissance began in Italy in the 1300s. Over the next two hundred years it spread all over Europe. The word "renaissance" means "new life." During the Renaissance there was newness in many areas of life. This marked an important change in human thought.

This change of thought later became known as humanism. Humanism talks about the importance of man and the wonderful things man can do. It puts man at the center of things. That leads to ideas of man and God that are very different from those given in the Bible.

The importance of the Renaissance was made greater because it was followed by the Enlightenment. The Enlightenment was also known as the Age of Reason. Many of the leaders of the Renaissance still said they believed in God. In the Enlightenment, though, many of the leaders said that there was no God. Even if there was a God, they said, He did not care about man. Men were left to find truth by themselves.

The mistake of the men of the Enlightenment was not in seeing the importance of human thinking. Their mistake was in putting human thinking in the place of God's commands. It was in rejecting anything they could not understand.

There have been two other things that have shaped how men think today. The first of these is the Industrial Revolution. The term "Industrial Revolution" is used to describe the period that began in England in 1760. It quickly spread to the rest of Europe and North America. Now it has spread to other parts of the world. In the Industrial Revolution men learned how to use power tools instead of hand tools. They started making things in great factories instead of in their homes. As a result fewer men were able to make many more things.

As a result of the Industrial Revolution, men began to think that they could make anything they wanted. They no longer felt a need for God.

The second thing that shaped how men think today is Darwinism. Charles Darwin's father planned that his son would become a minister of the gospel. In fact, young Charles did study to become a minister. Later he decided that no man could know God. He was not even sure there was a God. Darwin believed that God was not needed to explain how the world began. At first most people did not accept Darwin's ideas. After a time, though, more and more people began to agree with him.

The change in the way people think led men to believe that they could decide what was true. They could decide what was right and what was wrong. They did not need God.

The Two Ways of Thinking About Truth

As we have seen, there have been four things that have changed the way people think. These are the Renaissance, the Enlightenment, the Industrial Revolution and Darwinism. The change brought about by these four things has led to a new way of thinking about truth.

The old way of thinking about truth is that God decides what is true. This way is both objective and absolute. It applies to all people, at all times and in all places. God is the maker of all things. He rules over all things. He is truth. He is the only judge of what is right and what is wrong.

The new way of thinking about truth is that each person decides for himself. This way is neither objective nor absolute. Truth is true only some times, for some people, under some conditions. What one person thinks is true may not be true for another person. What he thinks is true for him today may not be true for him tomorrow. What he thinks is true for him in his present condition may not be true when his condition changes.

In the past most people in our culture accepted the old way of thinking about truth. Now most people accept the new way. That is especially true of our young people. That is why so many older people today do not understand younger people.

The Bible says of Christ, "All things are held together by Him" (Colossians 1:17). That is true when speaking of the world. It also is true in speaking of what a person thinks. God is what holds everything together. Knowing Him is what makes it possible for us to understand life. Without Him life is a mystery we cannot solve.

As Francis Schaeffer said, "If there is no absolute truth, then one cannot say in a final sense that anything is right or wrong. By absolute we mean that which is always true, that which is the final standard. There must be an absolute if there is to be right and wrong. . . . If there is no absolute, then there is nothing to make a final judgment between people whose ideas disagree."

As Time Goes By

It took many years for most people to accept the idea that God is not needed. For the most part, the ideas about the greatness of man just did not enter the thinking of the common man. As time went by, though, more and more people accepted the new ideas. After 1900 the change became more rapid. That was because of changes in communication and transportation. Those changes were not wrong in themselves. However, they did allow for the wider, more rapid spread of ideas. As a result the young people growing up now are being raised in a very different world from those who grew up in the early 1900s.

The Coming of the Mass Media

One of the greatest changes of the 1900s was the coming of the mass media. The "mass media" includes not only newspapers and magazines but also radio, movies, television and the Internet. Those who were born before 1927 can remember the first radios and talking movies. Those born between 1927 and 1945 can remember the first televisions. Most of those born between 1946 and 1964 cannot remember a time without television. Their children cannot imagine life without computer games and cell phones.

The mass media has changed our world in three important ways.

First, the mass media has made it possible for news and ideas to spread quickly. That makes the world seem smaller than ever before. Wars seem closer and problems far away seem more important. The mass media has brought us closer together with the people in other countries. This closeness has not helped people to understand what is right or what is wrong, however. Instead it has made it harder to judge between right and wrong.

Second, the mass media has changed the way family members connect with one another. Families used to talk around the dinner table. Now they watch television. Many young people watch television or movies or listen to music for hours every day. They spend less than four minutes a day talking with their mothers. Their fathers get only two-and-a-half minutes of their time. How can parents have much effect on their young people under those conditions? How can they teach them about truth? How can they influence them about right and wrong?

Third, the mass media does not present a true picture of life. It does not show the connection between actions and their results. Movie heroes solve problems in less than two hours. Television heroes do it in less than an hour. Usually they do it through fighting. That does not teach your children how to solve their own problems. Even more than that, the movies and television do not show God's idea of right and wrong. They show only man's ideas.

The Move to the City

During the 1900s the number of people moving from the farm to the city increased. This movement separated children from their larger families. It used to be that children grew up under the influence of their grandparents and other family members. By what they said and how they lived, those family members helped teach children about right and wrong. In the move to the city that help was often lost.

In the move to the city, children often lost the chance to learn to work. On the farm they worked with their fathers and mothers. They worked in the fields and took care of the animals together. They prepared food and cleaned house together. That working together taught important skills. It also gave time to talk and teach. In the city the fathers and mothers went off to work. The children were left with others who might not have the same values or concerns the parents had.

The move to the city also robbed children of the chance to learn that actions have results. On the farm each child was given important jobs to do. They learned early that if they did not milk the cow there would be no milk. If they did not gather eggs, there would be no eggs to eat. In the city the parents worked to earn money. Then they went to the store and bought the milk and eggs. The children had nothing to do with it.

Too Many Things

Another thing that has made our young people different from young people in earlier times is the problem of having too many things. Since the end of World War II most people in the West have experienced a great increase in the amount of money they have. That makes it possible for them to buy more things. Then they care more about what they have than about who they are.

Just 15 percent of the people born before 1927 thought that having a high-paying job was a desirable thing. That number increased to nearly 30 percent among their children. Among their children's children it went even higher. Money and the things money can buy became the most important thing to them. It became more important than the question of right and wrong. It became more important than God.

We should not be surprised that our young people feel this way. Ever since the 1950s most parents have said that they want their children to have the things they never had. These parents made providing for their families the most important thing. In doing so, they were too busy to teach their children how to judge between right and wrong.

The Increasing Influence of Public Schools

Public schools have been an important part of American culture for many years. At first that influence was for good. In recent years, though, three important changes have taken place.

First, the number of children in school increased rapidly following World War II. That forced our schools to change from neighborhood schools to education factories. Neighborhood schools were often taught by family members or neighbors. The

27

teachers knew the parents of each of the children. The things that were taught agreed with what the parents believed.

When the number of children increased, there was a need for more room and more teachers. Instead of adding rooms to many small schools, the government built larger schools that would serve several neighborhoods. These larger schools became education factories. Teachers were brought in from outside the neighborhoods. The teachers did not know the neighborhoods or what the people believed.

Second, there has been a growing influence of the government in the local schools. More and more the government decides what is to be taught instead of letting the local schools decide. In that way the parents have less control over what their children are being taught.

Third, parents have changed their thinking about the training of their children. Parents now expect the teachers to be responsible for the teaching of their children. That is true of parents with children in the public schools. It is also true of parents with children in private schools or Christian schools. This is happening at a time when teachers as well as church workers are crying for parents to be more involved in the education of their own children.

Meeting the Problem

These things have not caused the crisis of truth that troubles our young people today. They have only helped spread the ideas that began with the Renaissance. Things like television and the public schools are not the issue here. The issue is the way parents have reacted to the changes.

I know we cannot turn back the clock. We cannot go back to those days before television when most families lived on farms. I would not want to do that. This is an exciting time to be alive. But we can learn from history. We can understand why our culture changed. Then we can begin to react to the dangers in those changes. We can see how we failed to meet the great changes of the past hundred years. We can see how our failure has kept us from passing our beliefs on to our children. Then we will be better able to answer our culture.

At every turn we can fight against our culture's move away from dependence on God. If we do that, we will be in a better position to help our young people live true to the Bible.

Chapter 4

From Generation to Generation

The people were waiting for Pastor Milford to begin his Sunday morning sermon. He was uneasy, not sure how they would receive it. In the four years he had been pastor there, he had never cried when he preached. He was trying hard not to cry now.

"I come before you a different man than I was last Sunday," he began. "Several things have happened that have made me see how weak I am and how often I have failed to do what I should do.

"The book of Judges tells us that Joshua and the people of his generation were faithful to the Lord as long as they lived. They had seen the parting of the Red Sea and had eaten the bread God sent down from heaven. They had seen the other wonderful things God did for them after they left Egypt.

"Their children had not seen those mighty acts, but they had listened to the stories their fathers told. They had heard about how the mountain shook when God spoke to Moses on Mount Sinai. They had heard about when the walls of Jericho fell down. Because they had learned those stories well, they remained faithful to the Lord.

"The Bible says that the people were faithful as long as Joshua lived and as long as the children of the generation after Joshua lived. Something went wrong with the generation after that, though. The Bible says they did not know the Lord or what He had done for Israel. Because they did not know the Lord, they left Him and worshiped false gods.

"What went wrong? Oh, it is true that their way of life was very different from that of their parents. Their parents had grown up

31

while the Israelites were still living in the open. When they had come into the Promised Land, though, they moved into houses and made gardens. That is the life their children knew.

"In that new land their neighbors were Canaanites, Jebusites and Amorites. God had given the land to the Israelites because those other people were so evil. Many of those evil people had been destroyed, but many remained. But that was not the real problem."

Pastor Milford looked at his wife. Seventeen-year-old Philip sat on one side of her and nine-year-old Sarah sat on the other side. He looked at Gary and Penny Marsh with their three children. He looked at Geena Santoro, a single mother whose daughter had just gotten married.

"The reason that generation did not know the Lord is that their parents had said, 'I want to give my children the things I never had.' While they gave their children many material things, they did not do as their parents had done. They did not tell their children the stories of how God had brought them out of Egypt and provided for them in the wilderness. They failed to teach them why God's law is so important. They taught their children all about how to make a living, but they never found the time to teach them about God.

"The same things are happening today. Our children are being influenced less by their parents than they are by the culture. That culture does not know right from wrong. The result is a generation that does not know the Lord or what He has done for those who obey Him.

"Our children do not accept our values. We cannot blame the media. We cannot blame the culture. We cannot blame the government or the schools. They are not responsible to teach Bible truths to our children. We are. We must not expect to change our culture. We must, however, change the way we react to our culture. We must limit how much we allow the culture to affect us and our children."

Some of the people in the congregation began looking at each other. The pastor was sure some of them did not agree with him. Some even looked angry.

"The reason our children do not accept our values is not because of the condition of society. Our children do not accept our values because of how we parents have reacted to society. We have failed to give our children the spiritual guidance and teaching that would defend them against the effects of society. We have given up the job of teaching our children and have allowed others to do this. We do not even know the people who are teaching them. We do not know what our children are being taught."

The pastor was getting tired. "Most importantly, we cannot expect our children to be honest if we are not honest. We cannot expect them to obey the law if we do not obey the law. We cannot expect them to remain sexually pure if we are careless about our own sexual purity. We cannot expect them to have a good understanding of marriage if we leave our marriage when things get hard.

"We must accept the fact that it is our duty to teach our children right from wrong. It is not society's duty. It is not the school's duty. It is not even the church's duty. It is our duty to give our children a solid understanding of what the Bible teaches. We must prepare them to make good decisions in an evil world.

"We must take time with our children. We must sacrifice the things we want to do. We must teach them when they rise up, when they are in the way, and when they lie down to rest" (Deuteronomy 6:7).

The pastor closed his eyes and began to pray. "Father God, I come before you in sorrow. I am sorry for what I have done. I have failed my children. I have left it to the church to make them Christians. I have trusted the school to teach them. I have allowed the media to fill their time.

I had forgotten that 'children are a gift from the Lord' (Psalm 127:3). I had forgotten that my greatest duty is to raise my children in the teaching and fear of the Lord.

"Father, help me right now to begin to be serious about my duty to my children. Help me to see that I cannot expect some other person to do what is my duty to do. Help me to teach my children what the Bible says about how we should live. Help me to take whatever time is necessary with my children. Help me to make sure my children know You and the things You have done for me. Amen."

When he finished his prayer, Pastor Milford walked to the back of the church in silence. The people stood, quietly looking at one another. Then they, too, began moving toward the door.

The pastor stood at the door, shaking hands with the people as they left. Geena Santoro kept the pastor's hand in her own as she looked him in the eye. "I did not find much help in the house of God this morning," she said. "Some of us have done the best we could for our children under difficult conditions."

She seemed about to cry as she continued. "Pastor, you will never know how hard it is to be a single mother. I love my daughter, and I am proud of her. I raised her with very little help, and I think I did a good job. I take offense at your saying that I left my marriage when things got hard. I did what I had to do, what I thought was best at the time. That is all any of us can do."

The pastor listened thoughtfully as she spoke but said nothing.

As Geena talked to the pastor, the Marsh family drove away from the church. As they went they talked about the morning's service. Penny looked at her husband and asked, "What did you think of the sermon?"

Gary took a deep breath. "Well," he began.

Before he could continue, fifteen-year-old Brittney spoke from the backseat. "The pastor really got you about driving too fast, Dad."

"I think you missed his point," Gary said as he turned and smiled at his daughter. "He did not say that driving fast is wrong."

Seven-year-old Michael looked up from his place between his parents and asked, "He did not say that?"

"No," his father said. "He was just using that as an example." He saw that his wife was watching him closely as he continued. "He was saying that we need to teach our children right from wrong. I think we have done that."

"Sure!" Brittney said to eleven-year-old Lauren as the two sisters sank back into their seats.

Michael quietly turned to look out the window. Penny Marsh smiled at her husband, but she was not sure about what he had said. The rest of the trip home passed in silence.

Chapter 5
More True than False

Penny Marsh felt as though someone had hit her in the stomach. She had left work early to come home. The house was quiet. Penny looked at her watch. Brittney should be home from school by now. Penny walked up the stairs to Brittney's room and called her name. Then without waiting, she opened the door and looked in. She could hardly believe what she saw.

A naked boy rolled off the bed on to the floor. Brittney pulled up the blanket at her feet and quickly covered her own nakedness. Penny looked about the room in shock. She thought she was going to be sick. The boy's clothes lay at her feet. She kicked them toward him.

"Get out!" she screamed. She was surprised at how angry she sounded. But she screamed again, "Get out!"

The boy took up his clothes and held them in front of him as he left the room. He did not look at Brittney. Penny shook as she watched her oldest child. Brittney would not look at her.

Late that evening Brittney sat across from her mother and father. She and Penny had both been crying. Forty-two-year-old Gary Marsh was trying hard to control his anger.

"How long has this been going on?" Penny asked.

"Matt and I just started going out," Brittney answered.

"I do not mean just him. I mean you. Have you been with other boys?"

Brittney did not answer for a long time. Then she quietly said, "Yes." Penny began crying again.

"How many?" Gary asked.

"Why is that important?" Brittney answered as she finally raised her eyes to face her parents. "I have never had unprotected sex, if that is what you are concerned about. You act as though it is something to be ashamed of. Well, it is not! It is a way of showing love. What is wrong with that?"

"You lied to us!" Penny answered.

"And what would you have done if I had told you?" Brittney demanded.

Gary was standing now, looking down at Brittney. "How can you sit there and tell me that you do not see anything wrong with what you have done? You have been brought up in the church, Brittney Marsh! Has a Christian home not done anything for you?"

Brittney stood, too, and looked at her father. "Yes," she almost screamed. "It has taught me about love. I love Matt, and you cannot tell me that is wrong!"

Brittney left the room in anger. Her father watched her, not sure what to do. Finally, unable to decide, he sat down beside his wife. Penny said, "She is so young."

"Yes," Gary agreed, "but she is old enough to know better."

What Our Young People Think About Love and Sex

That tragic story is all too common. I often get calls and letters from heart-broken parents like Gary and Penny Marsh. I also hear from young people like Brittney.

George Barna of The Barna Research Group says that three out of four people born in the 1960s and 1970s had sex before marriage. That includes people who attend church as well as those who do not. Of all the babies born to that group in 1992, nearly half were born to women who were not married.

Our own study shows that children from Christian homes and good churches are being affected by society's interest in sex. By age eighteen, one in four church young people have had a sexual experience. More than half have taken part in touching breasts. They see no reason why such actions are wrong. Nearly half of the young people from good churches agree with Brittney that love makes sex right.

Truth Makes a Difference

When my children were very young, they enjoyed playing with a toy man. It had a round bottom with weight in it. My children would push him over and watch him spring back to a sitting position. Why did he do that? He did it because that is the way he was made.

Strong beliefs will do for our children just what the round bottom and weight did for that toy man. Strong belief in the truths of God will always return them to a right position. That will be true even when a sinful society tries its hardest to tempt them to do wrong. Without the weight of truth, though, our children do not know which way is right or which way is wrong.

We cannot promise that a strong belief in absolute truth will keep our young people from sexual experiences before marriage. But our children are much more likely to think that sex before marriage is right if they do not have a strong belief in absolute truth. Most who think that way will become sexually active. Our study shows that the most important thing we can do for our young people is to give them solid training in the truths of the Bible.

Beth reached across the coffee shop table and took Geena's hand.

"I am sorry," Geena said through her tears. "I am so ashamed." Beth McConnell and Geena Santoro had been friends for a long time. They had been meeting for coffee every Tuesday morning for several years. That weekly meeting began when Geena's daughter went away to attend a small Christian school. There she met a fine young art student and married at the age of twenty.

"What is wrong, Geena?" Beth asked kindly. She waited while Geena dried her tears.

"Melissa called last night," Geena answered in a voice that shook. "She and Don are getting a divorce." Geena saw Beth's face change. "Oh, do not look at me like that," Geena continued. "You do not know how many times I have wondered if I did the right thing leaving Kenneth. But I hoped I could keep my daughter from making the same mistakes I made.

"I begged Melissa to try to work things out with Don. But she said it is just not working out. I told her to give it some time. 'You have been married for only seven or eight months,' I said. 'Don has been in his new job for only a few months.' Finally I said, 'Go and see a counselor.' She said, 'It would not do any good.' I just do not know what to tell her."

Geena was hoping her friend would understand and share her hurt. But Beth's face was set, her mouth closed firmly as she looked at her friend. She said nothing for a long time.

Finally Beth said, "I do not judge you, Geena. I am sorry I never told you. My Richard is separated from his wife. They see a counselor every week." Her voice was strained and she was beginning to cry.

For a long time they held each other's hands without speaking. At last Geena said, "What is wrong with us, Beth? Why can we not stay married? Why are so many families torn to pieces?"

40

How Our Young People See Marriage and Family

Beth and Geena's experiences are not unusual. In recent years our society has changed how people think of the family. Many people have said that the old ideas of marriage and family are no longer true. They speak of "open marriages" or of "marriages" between two men or between two women.

Recent studies, though, have shown that most people still believe in marriage and the family. Most men and women in the United States still believe that divorce is wrong. They want a happy marriage. They believe that good families are important to the health of the nation. It is not just Christians who feel that way. People who are not Christians agree.

In many ways most of our church young people agree with their parents about marriage and family. Nine out of ten agree that God's plan is for marriages to last a lifetime. Of those young people who have had sexual relations before marriage, three out of five wish they had not. Most of our young people say they know their parents love each other and their children. Yet less than half of them say they want a marriage like their parents' marriage.

Two out of three of our young people say it is all right for parents to divorce if they no longer love each other. They say parents should not stay married just because of their children.

How They Understand "Family"

A recent study by The Barna Research Group shows a change in what people mean by the word "family." In the past most people thought that "family" meant a group of people who were connected to one another by birth, marriage or adoption.

Today many people understand "family" to mean a group of people who care deeply about one another. That means the group is united only by feelings. When a person no longer cares about someone, he or she is no longer part of his family. Family

41

is no longer based on either man's law or God's law. Such a family can be always changing. When things get hard, as they sometimes do, people can just leave.

This idea has been presented to our young people at school, in the media and by their friends. Three out of five of our young people have accepted it. Only one in three of our young people still accepts the older meaning of "family." That means that most of our young people understand "family" to include two or more people who are not married living together. This idea would say that two men or two women living together would make a family.

Why Truth Is Important

Our study shows that what our children believe about truth will shape how they think about marriage and family. That can make the difference between a life of happiness or a life of sorrow. It can provide what a child needs to choose between what is right and what only seems to be right.

For example, those young people who have a strong belief in absolute truth are more likely to believe that God meant marriage to last a lifetime. They are more likely to say their family experiences are good. They are more likely to want to save sex until marriage. They are more likely to say that if there are children involved the parents should not get divorced even if they no longer love each other. They are much more likely to consider strong families as an important part of the health of a society.

Young people who do not have a strong belief in absolute truth are more likely to believe it is all right for an unmarried man and woman to live together. They are much more likely to believe it is all right for two men or two women to consider themselves married to each other.

This means that if our children do not have a strong belief in absolute truth they will think marriage is not necessary. They may even think marriage is a bad thing.

42

What our children think about marriage and family will decide how they will live. Our girls will be more likely to live with a boy without marriage. If they marry at all, they will do so with a completely different way of thinking. Divorce will come to their minds as soon as they have a problem in their marriage.

If we want to prepare our children for lifelong marriage, we must teach them the absolute truths of the Bible. We must teach them how to put those truths to use in their lives.

———————

Pastor James Milford walked with his son to the school counselor's office. As they walked he put his hand on Philip's shoulder. In anger, Philip shook it off.

"Good morning, Mr. Milford," the woman in the office said. "How are you, Philip?" Philip did not answer.

"Are you ready to come back to school?" she asked. Still he did not answer.

The woman turned to Pastor Milford. "Thank you," she said. "We will take it from here."

Later that day Pastor Milford sat in his office with Carl Strickland, an officer of the church. He was telling about his son's return to school after being made to stay out for four days. "Philip is still not happy with me," he finished.

"I know your boy had to miss some days of school," Strickland said. "But you have not told me everything, have you?"

Pastor Milford took a deep breath. He looked very tired, like a man much older than he was. "Philip got caught cheating on a test at school," he explained.

Strickland thought he understood. "We have all faced that, James," he said. "Young people all go through it sooner or later."

"No," Pastor Milford said. "This is not just something all young people go through." He changed his position in his chair before beginning his story. Mrs. Brewster had caught Philip cheating on an important test. She ordered him to follow her out of the room. There she talked to him about how bad it was for him to cheat. Then she told him to follow her back into the room. She would write a note to the principal and he must take it to the principal's office.

At that, Philip became angry. He said he would go to the principal's office but he would not go back into the room. He did not want to face the looks of the other students. When Mrs. Brewster demanded that he go with her, Philip became more angry and began talking very loudly. He began calling her bad names and pushed her against the wall.

That is when someone caught him from behind. It was Mr. Detweiler, a teacher from another room. Mr. Detweiler took Philip to the principal's office and left him there.

"But that is not what troubles me most, Carl," Pastor Milford said. "That afternoon the school counselor called to tell me what had happened. I went to the school and brought him home. We talked in the car on the way home. I was angry. I said, 'Philip, what got into you? Cheating on a test is bad enough, but attacking your teacher like that!'

"Then he lied to me. He tried to tell me that the teacher just did not like him. He said he had not cheated. He started to make up a story about how it all happened. That is when I really got angry.

"I told him his counselor had given me the notes he had used to cheat. I told him that she had told me the things he said to his teacher. I told him it was worse than anything I had ever had to listen to in my life.

44

"I said, 'How do you think that makes me look? The pastor's son cheating on a test and attacking a teacher! Is that the way you want people to think of your family? I am ashamed to be your father.' Then before he got out of the car, I said, 'That is no way for a Christian to act.'

"As he left the car, he said, 'I never said I was a Christian!'"

The two men looked at each other in silence.

"You know what the hardest part of all this is, Carl?" the pastor finally continued. "He was right. I had never thought about it before, but Philip had never really come to faith in Christ. He has gone to Sunday school and church all his life. But as he said, he has never said he was a Christian. I have to admit that I have never tried to lead my son to Christ."

"Even our children have to choose for themselves," Carl offered.

"That is not what I am talking about. I am not talking about what I learned about my son. I am talking about what I learned about myself. This past week I have talked with Philip about things we have never talked about before. I have always told him many things about how he should act. You know that. Probably everyone in the church knows that."

"You have always been firm with your children," Carl said. "That is not necessarily bad."

"Last Saturday, though, we began to talk, I mean really talk. I listened some of the time instead of always talking. I could not believe some of the things that were coming out of my son's mouth! He said he believes the Bible but he does not believe that the world was made as the Bible says. He said he thinks Christianity is all right but that Islam and other religions are just as good. He said he thinks that Satan is not real but is just a way of talking about all the evil in the world."

Carl Strickland seemed about to say something, but Pastor Milford hurried on.

"My point is that all this has made me understand that sending my son to Sunday school is not enough. If I have not given my son a biblical way of looking at life, Sunday school is not likely to have the effect on him that I want it to have."

How Our Young People Think About Faith and Religion

We cannot be sure that our children will accept Christian beliefs just because they are raised in Christian homes and taught in Christian churches. We cannot be sure that they will become Christians themselves.

If we are Christians, certainly we want our children to become Christians. More than that, as a man "thinks in his heart, so is he," as the Bible says (Proverbs 23:7). Beliefs lead to actions. And actions have effects.

Our study shows that three out of four young people who attend Christian youth groups have trusted Christ for their salvation. Yet many of them are unsure about the truths of the Bible. They are unsure about how to answer questions about God, the Bible, Satan, heaven, hell or salvation. Often they have to confess that they do not know.

Yet four out of five of these same young people agree that a person can know God in a personal way. Seven out of ten agree that the Christian faith is important to the way they live their lives. But they seem to be completely unable to compare Bible beliefs with other religions and ways of life. Four out of ten say that no one can prove which religion is really true.

Many of these church young people believe all religions worship the same god. They believe that all good people will go to heaven when they die.

46

Truth and Believers

Our study shows a connection between belief in objective truth and the spiritual life. That is, young people who have a firm understanding of objective truth are much better prepared in spiritual things. They are much more likely to attend Sunday school and church youth group every week. They are more likely to read the Bible and pray every day. They are more likely to believe that the Bible is completely true.

Young people who accept objective truth are more likely to become Christians. They are more likely to say they expect to go to heaven when they die because they have trusted in Jesus. They are more likely to see the connection between their faith and the way they live. They believe that Satan and hell are real. These young people accept that Jesus is the only way to God and heaven. They do not believe that a person can get to heaven just by doing enough good things.

What our young people think about sex, family and religion will decide how they choose to live their lives. Helping them learn the truths of the Bible at an early age will help them do what is right in later years.

How do we teach them the truths of the Bible about sex, family and religion? How do we help them accept objective truth? It begins with the Test of Truth.

Chapter 6

The Test of Truth

Penny Marsh was trying hard not to cry as she watched her daughter. So many things had happened since she had surprised Brittney while with a boy a week ago. Penny and Gary had spent hours crying together. It seemed that every day they had an angry talk with Brittney. Gary would get angry, Brittney would rebel and Penny would cry.

Now the three of them were sitting together. The younger children had been sent to a neighbor's house to play.

"Brittney, I promised you that this would not be like those other talks we have had," her father began. "I really do not want to be angry with you anymore."

There was a silence. Then Gary continued, "I just want some answers." He began to ask questions to which she quietly gave short answers. For the first time in a week they seemed to be talking together instead of fighting.

"How do you feel after you have gone to bed with a boy?"

"I have no idea."

"Do you feel guilty?"

"No."

"Because you do not think it is wrong?"

"No. Sometimes I feel sad."

"Why?"

"How would I know?"

As they continued talking Penny watched Brittney's face. Sometimes she thought she did not even know her own daughter. Other times she saw in Brittney her baby of fifteen years before.

Finally Brittney asked her father, "Why do you think it is wrong?"

"What do you mean?"

"If I love Matt, why is it wrong for me to sleep with him? If love makes it right for you and Mom, why is it wrong for me and Matt?"

Gary was shocked. "I cannot believe this!" he said. "Your mother and I are married! That is why it is different for us!"

"Why?" she asked. "Why does that make it different?"

"You know sex before marriage is wrong. You have been taught that all your life."

Penny, sitting on the arm of Gary's chair, pressed his arm to remind him of his promise not to get angry.

"Look," he said, trying to control his anger. "Some things are right and some things are wrong. You and I both know that what you are doing with Matt is wrong."

Brittney was getting angry now, too. "You may think it is wrong, but I do not. You have a right to your opinion, and I have a right to mine. Things are different from when you were young, you know!" She got up and started walking out of the room.

"Brittney Marsh, you get right back here," Gary demanded.

"I have to get ready for the ballgame."

Gary looked at his wife as he fell back into his chair. She looked at him, and this time she was not crying.

"You promised her this talk would be different," Penny said.

Gary only closed his eyes and wondered how things like ballgames could go on when things were so wrong in his family.

She Thinks She Is Right

Gary and Penny Marsh want the same thing for their children that you and I want for our children. We want them to believe that certain things are right and other things are wrong. We want them to choose right. The Marshes know that Brittney is choosing wrong. However, they do not know how to influence her to choose right.

Brittney thinks she is right. Even though she is choosing wrong, she still believes in truth. Every one believes in truth or they would never ask any questions, as Charles Sanders Pierce said.

We just know that some things are right and some things are wrong. For example, let Brittney discover that someone has taken her shoes. She would not say that that person has a right to his opinion. She would say that he was wrong to take something that did not belong to him.

Remember that there are two ways of thinking about truth. The first way is that God decides what is true. This way is both objective and absolute. The second way is for each person to decide for himself. This way is neither objective nor absolute. I have met many people like Brittney who say they accept the second way of thinking about truth. But I have never met a young person who did not expect to be treated fairly.

For many people accepting that there is a real right and a real wrong is not the problem. Their problem is how to know when something is wrong. The question we need to answer is, What truths are right for all people, for all times and for all places? Brittney certainly did not agree with her father on where the line between right sex and wrong sex should be drawn. She drew the line at "love." Her father drew it at "marriage."

Like Brittney, most young people believe that ideas of right and wrong are just opinions. If we do not agree with them, we should be able to prove that a thing is either right or wrong. What we need is a two-step test. First, we must compare an act or way of thinking with a rule that is both absolute and objective. Second, we need to be able to show how that rule works in real life.

Truth Compared to the Standard

In France there is an office called the International Bureau of Weights and Measures. Its job is to establish the correct metric measurements for the whole world.

Imagine that you and I did not agree about the length of a piece of wood you asked me to cut for you. I said it was the right length, but you said it was too short. How could we decide who was right? We could measure the piece of wood by a measuring stick that agreed with the one in the International Bureau of Weights and Measures.

That is just what our children need. They need to know that there is a measuring stick, or a standard, for deciding if a thing is right or wrong. That measuring stick exists outside of ourselves. That is, it is objective. To decide about an action, we must see how the action compares with that objective standard. First, though, we need to ask, What is that standard? Who made it?

God in the Story

A few years before Jesus was born, there was a Roman named Horace. He wrote stories. He said that the other men who wrote stories did not work hard enough. Instead of working out the hard problems in their stories, they brought in a god to do that for them. Horace said, "Do not bring a god into the story unless the problem is one that needs a god to solve it."

The problem of helping us tell right from wrong is one that needs God to solve it. In fact, only God can solve it. Only God can give us a measuring stick that will show how right and wrong are different. We cannot make such a measuring stick ourselves. If we did, it would not be objective. If we based it only on our experience, it could not be used by all people.

Many parents are like Gary Marsh. They think, "Some things are just right, and some things are just wrong." But we must do more than tell our children that some things are just right and some things are just wrong. We must give them the tools for deciding what things are wrong and why they are wrong. We must help them understand that some things are wrong because there is a holy God. Only that holy God can decide what is right and what is wrong.

The reason we think some things are fair and some things are not fair is that God is a fair God. The reason love is right and hate is wrong is that God is a God of love. The reason telling the truth is right and lying is wrong is that God is true. The reason sex within marriage is right and sex outside of marriage is wrong is that God is pure.

Many of our young people cannot tell right from wrong because their parents do not use God's measuring stick. Like Gary Marsh, they may say something is wrong because it is wrong. That is not enough. We must understand that it is what God is that makes a thing right. It is what God is not that makes a thing wrong. When a person chooses wrong, he is not just disagreeing with another person's opinion. He is disagreeing with the very nature of God.

The Beginning of Wisdom

It is best if children are taught these truths at an early age. But how can a very young child understand such great ideas? Once our children have gotten as old as Brittney Marsh, they have learned the wrong ideas from society. Then how can they be led to accept God as the standard of all things?

We must begin by teaching our very young children to fear God in the right way. We must teach them to accept His power and nature. As Solomon said, "The fear of the Lord is the beginning of wisdom" (Proverbs 9:10). Without knowing and fearing Him, we can never learn the difference between right and wrong.

I am afraid that many parents do not fear God as they should. When Moses came to the bush that was on fire, he heard the voice of God saying, "Take your shoes off your feet. For the place where you are standing is holy ground" (Exodus 3:5). Moses did what God told him. He fell on his knees and covered his face from the sight of God.

God once showed Himself to Isaiah in a dream. Isaiah cried, "It is bad for me, for I am destroyed! Because I am a man whose lips are unclean. And I live among a people whose lips are unclean. For my eyes have seen the King, the Lord of All" (Isaiah 6:5).

The Apostle John had known Jesus. He had walked the dusty roads with Him before His death. When John saw Jesus after He came back from the dead, he "fell down at His feet like a dead man" (Revelation 1:17).

Those men feared God. When I talk about fearing God, though, I do not mean being afraid of Him as we would be afraid of a wild animal. God is not some terrible being. We should not want to run from Him. The fear of God is a deep sense of His holiness. It is a feeling of wonder for who He is and what He can do.

Some time ago I was in South Africa to talk to Muslims about the Christian faith. In one of my talks, I said that God always acts in agreement with His holy nature. After I finished a young Muslim came to me. "Your idea of God is not my idea of Allah," he said. "Allah is all-powerful. Allah can do anything he wants to do."

54

"Can Allah cheat and lie?" I asked.

"Yes," he answered. "Allah can do anything. He is not limited like your God. If Allah wants to love, he loves. If he wants to hate, he hates."

"Could Allah punish you for something you did even if it was good?" I asked.

"If Allah did not like it, he would punish me."

"Then you do not always know what Allah might do to you, do you?"

He thought about that a little. Then he said, "No, I do not always know what he might do." He was silent for only a little more before he went on, "But I do know Allah is all-powerful."

"If I served Allah," I said, "I would be serving him out of fear. If he would punish me for doing good, he would be punishing me to satisfy his own desires. I would never know what would make him angry." He was listening carefully, so I continued. "I serve God out of love. Because God is holy and all-powerful, I fear Him. But because I understand that He is a loving God, I can serve Him out of love. I always know what will make God angry. I always know what will please Him."

We always know what will anger God and what will please Him. Fear keeps us from making Him angry. Love makes us want to please Him.

We should fear God because He is greater than any man. We often honor those who can do things we cannot do. We honor a man such as Albert Einstein for his great mind. We honor Sandra Day O'Connor because she was the first woman to serve on the highest court in the land. We honor Michael Jordon because of his great skill in sports. Yet God is greater than any of these. God is greater than man in holiness and power. He is greater in wisdom and love.

We should fear God because all good things come from Him. The Bible says, "Whatever is good and perfect comes to us from God" (James 1:17). He has everything we need. All that we are, He has made us. All that we have, He has given us. All that we do not have, He can provide. Think about how it would affect our children if they really believed that.

We should fear God because He alone is the judge of good and evil. The Bible says, "For God will judge every act, even everything which is hidden, both good and bad" (Ecclesiastes 12:14). He will measure every act against Himself. If it agrees with His own nature, it is good and right. If it does not agree with His own nature, it is evil.

We should fear God because He holds the power of life and death. God says, "It is I Who kills and gives life" (Deuteronomy 32:39).

We should fear God for our own good. God promises blessing for those who fear Him. He says, "I will give them one heart and one way, that they may fear Me always, for their own good and for the good of their children after them" (Jeremiah 32:39).

It is that fear of the Lord that we must recapture in ourselves, in our families and in our churches. We must have a holy fear of Him. The fear of the Lord must be in our mouths. It must be in the stories we tell our children. It must be in the way we think. Then we will be able to understand how we should live.

First Teachings of Right and Wrong
We must teach our children to fear the Lord. We must also teach them how His commands grow out of His nature. This is seen in the very first words God ever spoke to man. God told Adam, "You are free to eat from any tree of the garden. But do not eat

from the tree of learning of good and bad. For the day you eat from it you will die for sure" (Genesis 2:16-17).

Adam and Eve already understood the idea of good. All around them were things that God had said were good. Now they were forced to choose between good and evil. God drew a line around that tree that clearly marked the difference between right and wrong. In this way God showed Himself to be the One who decides what is right and what is wrong.

After Eve and her husband had eaten of the tree of learning of good and evil, God spoke to her. He said, "What is this you have done?" (Genesis 3:13). That is how God showed Himself to be the One who would judge between right and wrong. Because Adam and Eve had chosen to do evil, He punished them.

Through the whole Bible God shows that absolute truth comes only from Him. To Noah He showed Himself as the One Who blesses those who do right and punishes those who do evil. To Abraham He showed Himself to be the God who keeps promises. To David He showed Himself to be a God of mercy. In Jesus Christ He showed Himself to be the God of love that is beyond our understanding.

The Ten Commandments are the most famous words of absolute truth ever written. But we must understand why God gave the Ten Commandments. He gave them to the nation of Israel for two reasons. First, He gave them to show what kind of God He is. Second, He gave them so that the people could enjoy the blessings of choosing right.

For example, the first commandment says, "Have no gods other than Me" (Exodus 20:3). God knew that "all the gods of the nations are false gods. But the Lord made the heavens" (Psalm 96:5). The sixth commandment says, "Do not kill" (Exodus 20:13). God wanted people to understand that He is the One who gives life. The ninth commandment says, "Do not tell a lie" (Exodus 20:16). God wanted people to understand that He is truth. "He cannot lie" (Titus 1:2).

The Ten Commandments point to God's nature. They flow from Who He is. That is why they are true for all people, for all times and for all places.

Truth Is Based on God

The first thing we must do in order to prepare our young people to choose to do right is to teach them to fear God. The second thing we must do is to help them understand that all truth is based on Him.

For example, some people defend the importance of a rule by saying, "Because I say so!" Others will say, "Because the Bible says so!" Some will agree with Gary Marsh and say, "Because it is right!" Such answers will not satisfy everyone in every situation, though. That is why we need to teach our young people that an action is right because "God is like that." We need to teach them that an action is wrong because "God is not like that."

Some time ago I watched a popular movie with my thirteen-year-old daughter, my seventeen-year-old son and his girlfriend. The movie showed how the Nazis murdered six million Jews during World War II. After the movie I asked my son, "Do you believe it was wrong to kill so many people?"

He immediately answered, "Yes."

"Almost everyone would agree," I said. "But could they explain why it was wrong?"

I could see that all three young people were thinking hard about my question. I continued, "Most people believe that whatever most of the people of a society think is right is right. That is why so many people in America do not think abortion is wrong. But there is a problem with that. If that is true, how can we say that killing six million Jews was wrong?

"In fact, that is just what the Nazis said after the war to defend their actions. They said, 'How can you say we did wrong when our society agreed that it was right?' The world court said that the Nazis were wrong, though. The court said that there is something beyond society that decides right and wrong."

I went on to explain that today most people decide what is right or wrong based on what they think is best for themselves. "If we do not blame the Nazis for what they did," they think, "what will stop some other group from doing the same to us?" Their thinking is good, but it does not lead to a full understanding of right and wrong. They cannot find a full understanding of right and wrong because they leave God out.

After we had talked for a long time, I thought it was time to lead the young people to the truth. "Do you know why what you saw tonight was wrong?" I asked.

"I know it was wrong," my son said, "but I cannot say why it was wrong."

I explained, "There is a truth about killing that is far above ourselves. It comes from the nature of God. Killing is wrong because there is a living God. He made life and said, 'It is good.' He commanded us not to kill."

That night I strengthened the understanding of those young people that right and wrong come from the nature of God. Without God there can be no absolute right and wrong.

The Plan for Teaching Truth

The way of thinking I gave those young people can be used in other areas of life. Lying is wrong because God is true. Stealing is wrong because God is just. Hate is wrong because God is love. These things are not wrong because society thinks they are wrong. They are not wrong because the church thinks they are wrong. They are wrong because they are in conflict with the nature of God.

It is hard to teach such things to young people who have grown up in the ways of a godless society. How can we do it? We must do it in the same way we teach anything. We must start with simple truths and develop from there. That is why God began teaching the children of Israel with ten simple commands. When they learned those, they could learn other truths based on those commands. That is God's plan for teaching truth.

Picture the Test of Truth

God's Word is filled with Commands or Rules, put there for our good. These Rules grow from Basic Truths. The Basic Truths grow from the Person of God Himself.

To make this easy to understand, look at the tree in the picture. Think of Rules as the leaves and branches, Basic Truths as the trunk, and the roots growing from God Himself. They are all naturally connected.

As we look from Rules to Basic Truths, they lead us to God Himself. As we look to God Himself, He leads us to Basic Truths and on to Rules. With the Test of Truth we are able to compare our thoughts, ideas, and actions to God's nature and what He is like.

Rule

When you first went to school, you spent many hours learning such things as two plus two makes four. Those were your first small steps in the study of numbers. You may have been pleased with your new skills. You did not understand, however, all that would follow in the coming years.

In the same way most people do not understand when they begin to study the Bible just where that study will take them. God said, "Do not kill" and "Do not have a desire for your neighbor's house" (Exodus 20:13, 17). He said, "Do not say bad things against a man who cannot hear. Do not put something in the way of a man who cannot see" (Leviticus 19:14). He gave clear commands like a parent telling a child not to touch the fire. He did that to show us how we should treat each other.

God's commands, though, do not just tell us what is right and what is wrong. They also point to a larger truth. The Apostle Paul wrote that God's law leads us by the hand, like a child being led to school. In school he will learn even greater things (Galatians 3:24).

In Paul's day many homes had a slave called the paidagogos. The paidagogos was in charge of a child's training. He was not the teacher, but he would take the child to school and place him under the care of the teacher. Paul was saying that is just the way the law leads us to God. By seeing the kinds of commands God gives, we come to understand what kind of God He is.

Basic Truth

Behind each command of God there is a Basic Truth. A Basic Truth is a truth that can be seen in more than one kind of situation. It is the truth on which a command or rule is based. It explains the "why" behind a command.

That is what Brittney Marsh was looking for in her talk with her father. He was able to make her understand that her parents did not want her to have sex. What she did not understand was the Basic Truth that lay behind that rule. When she asked her father to explain why her actions were wrong, he was not able to do so. A concern for safety is one of the Basic Truths behind a mother's command to look both ways before crossing the street. Concern for life is the Basic Truth behind the command, "Do not kill."

Honesty is the Basic Truth behind the command, "Do not tell a lie about your neighbor."

We must prepare our young people to use the Test of Truth in choosing between right and wrong. We begin to do so by showing them the Basic Truths behind God's commands. But behind the Basic Truths is the very Person of God Himself.

What does it mean?

Person of God: the nature of God, what God is like, what God is. For example, God is love, faithful, pure, and true. These are not only things He does; they are what He is.

Person of God

It is useless to know the Basic Truths that lie behind God's laws if we do not know God Himself. Too often we study God's law without even thinking about Him. But He shows Himself to us in His laws so that we might get to know Him. He plans that we should move from rules to Basic Truth then to knowing God.

Moses understood this plan. The Bible says that God spoke with Moses "face to face" (Exodus 33:11). After that Moses said, "If I have found favor in Your eyes, let me know Your ways. Then I may know You" (Exodus 33:13). He knew that understanding God's rules and the Basic Truths behind those rules would lead him to knowing God.

Many people do not like to read the parts of Exodus and Leviticus that tell about Old Testament worship. They think that those things have nothing to do with us in these days. But all those things show the nature of God. For example, those books say many things about purity. That is because God is pure. Those books say much about sin because God is holy.

In Psalm 19 David used a number of words to describe God's law. He said God's law is perfect, sure, right, pure, clear, true and righteous. Those things are true of God's law because they
62

are true of Him. The truth does not come from the law; it comes from God. Those things were in God before He gave the law. They were in God before He made the world. They are true forever because God is without beginning or ending.

The truth flows out of the nature of God into His laws. That is why it is right for all people, for all times and for all places. Today's young people, though, may not be ready to accept that truth. They say they want something that is real. That is why parents and youth leaders must take the next step and have them judge truth by asking, "Does it really work?"

Chapter 7

The Evidence of Truth

Pastor Milford and his wife were just putting their purchases into their car. Geena Santoro called out as she walked toward him. "I want to apologize for the way I received your sermon last Sunday," she said. She stopped, but it was clear that she had more she wanted to say.

He gave her time to continue. She told about her talk with her daughter. As she talked, the pastor became more and more concerned. He had married Don and Melissa. "Anyway," Geena finished, "I just wanted to say I am sorry for acting the way I did."

The pastor smiled a little as he said, "You are not the only one who was angry about that sermon. I know I spoke very strongly, but I meant to. I was speaking as much to myself as I was to other people. I have been taking a serious look at the kind of father I have been."

"I did not do a very good job with Melissa, either," Geena said.

"Oh, that is not what I mean, Geena. All of us could have done better. Not any of us can be sure that our children will live the way we would like for them to live. But what I have been thinking is, have I done everything I could to prepare my children to face the world? I have decided that I have failed to do some of the most important things for my children."

Geena was becoming more interested. "What things?" she asked.

Pastor Milford told how he had been trying to help his son. "I have been trying to show him that the idea of right and wrong is based on what God is like. A thing is not right just because I say so. It is right because God is the way He is."

"Has it had any effect?" she asked.

"I think Philip understands what I am saying. But I am not sure he accepts it. These things take time, though. Maybe we could get together sometime in the next few days. That way my wife and I could have more time to tell you what the Lord has been teaching us. We can probably learn a few things from you, too."

"I would like that," Geena said. She started to walk away but turned back. "Would it be all right if I invite some other people? I have talked with several other parents about your sermon. I think they are interested in the kind of thing you are talking about."

Why Look at the Evidence of Truth?

The Test of Truth is hard for some young people to accept. If they do not trust the Bible, they will not look to it for guidance. If they do not believe that God is a God of love, it will be hard for them to accept the nature of God as the base of truth.

The Test of Truth is a good place to start with young children. With young people, though, the Evidence of Truth is a better place to start. Most young people say that they do not believe in absolute truth. The Evidence of Truth will help them re-examine that idea. That may lead them to accept the Bible as the only standard for making right choices.

Truth Agrees with Reality

Our young people want to know if truth works in everyday life. Does it make any difference in the way they live? Does truth help them live a better life? Those are the questions the Evidence of Truth tries to answer. It shows how the Test of Truth works in the real world and how truth agrees with reality.

Brittney Marsh told her parents, "You have a right to your opinion, and I have a right to mine." She was saying that there is no way to tell which opinion is right and which is wrong. Her parents needed to give her clear evidence that God's direction on sex is the right one. Brittney needed to see the Evidence of Truth.

Cruel Rules

Rules may seem cruel until we understand the reason for them. A young child may not understand why he must not play in a busy street. Because he does not understand, he may cry or disobey his parents. When he is older he will understand how much a car or truck could hurt him. Then he will be thankful for the limits his parents placed on him.

Many people feel about God's laws the way that young child feels about his parents' rule. They think God is keeping them from enjoying the fun things of life. They do not understand that God's laws are given for their own safety. They do not understand that God does not hate us. He loves us. Because He loves us, He wants us to be safe and happy.

God gave such commands as "Have nothing to do with sexual sin" (1 Corinthians 6:18). He did not give those commands to make our lives hard. He gave them because He knew some things we did not know. For example, He knew that sexual sin is not the way to fun and satisfaction. It is the way of disappointment and defeat.

Moses understood this when he wrote, "And now, Israel, what does the Lord your God ask of you? He wants you to fear the Lord your God, to walk in all His ways and love Him. He wants you to serve the Lord your God with all your heart and all your soul. He wants you to keep all the laws of the Lord *which I am telling you today for your good"* (Deuteronomy 10:12-13, my emphasis).

God gave His commands for our good! He looks down from where He sits and sees things we cannot see. He gives us laws to protect us and provide for us. We need to remind our young people of this over and over again. We must teach them that all truth comes from the nature of God for their good.

As Bill Hybels writes,

> The Lord tells us that His commands are not hard to obey (I John 5:3). By that He does not mean that they are easy to keep. Instead he is telling us that they are never foolish. They are never unnecessary. They are never without purpose. He does not give us rules which are of no value.
>
> Every rule in the Bible was made with great wisdom. Each one was made both to honor God and to help us. The whole book of Deuteronomy shows this. In that book Moses again and again said that God gave the commands for our good. God promises to bless us if we obey them.

Jeremiah wrote, "'For I know the plans I have for you,' says the Lord, 'plans for well-being and not for trouble, to give you a future and a hope'" (Jeremiah 29:11). A little later He said, "That they may fear me always, for their own good and for the good of their children after them" (Jeremiah 32:39).

Choosing right instead of wrong does not take all the fun out of life. In fact, it works for our good because absolute truth is based on the nature of God. He loves us, and He knows what is best for us.

Most young people agree that God set the limits for men. They believe that bad things will happen to people who do not obey God's laws. Yet they do not connect that belief to their own actions. The Evidence of Truth will help our young people make that connection.

A Warning

We must be careful when talking about bad things happening to people who disobey God's laws. Bad things also happen to people who obey God. Neither can we say that people who disobey are never happy. That is not true. In fact Jeremiah asked, "Why does the way of the sinful go well?" (Jeremiah 12:1).

The Evidence of Truth does not say that right choices always bring good things. Neither does it say that wrong choices always bring bad things. It simply says that God's laws form a cover of protection over us. The wise person will want to stay under that cover. Remember that sin always promises immediate satisfaction. Sometimes it even keeps that promise. Some of the results of that sin may not come in this life, but they will come.

Also, we must be careful that we do not give the idea that God's laws are true because they lead to good results. Let me explain what I mean. Some of the things I learned in my early years of school have been very helpful to me. But they are not true because they are useful. They are true because they agree with what is real. They remain true even if I never get any help from them.

The Evidence of Truth can help your young people tell the difference between right and wrong. Then they will be prepared to choose the right.

We can trust God's commands to do two things for us. They protect and provide.

Seeking God's Protection

I once knew a young man I will call Greg. He lived near a family that had a large swimming pool behind their house. There was a high wall around the pool to keep people out. Greg did not know the family and so he was never invited to use the pool.

One dark night when Greg knew his neighbors were not home, he and his girlfriend decided to go swimming. While his girlfriend was still removing her shoes, Greg ran to the pool and jumped in head first. His girlfriend cried out, but it was too late. There was very little water in the pool. When Greg hit the bottom of the pool, he was badly injured. In fact, his injury was so bad that he was never able to walk again.

Greg and his girlfriend had climbed over the wall around the pool. He probably thought it was there only to keep him from having fun. In fact, it was there for his protection. His failure to honor that wall cost him more than he wanted to pay. In the same way, there is a high cost for us when we fail to honor the walls God has built for our protection.

Many years ago Dr. S.I. McMillen wrote a book called *None of These Diseases*. There he shows how God's commands serve to protect us from many diseases. McMillen wrote: "When God led the Israelites out of Egypt, He promised them that if they obeyed His commands, He would put 'none of these diseases' upon them. God promised a freedom from disease that modern medicine cannot give."

God's commands are for our protection. When we place ourselves outside of His protection, we must pay the cost.

Seeking God's Provision

When my children were young, I took them to the Great Smoky Mountains National Park. One morning we set out to walk to the top of Clingman's Dome, the highest point in the park. It was a long walk, and we got tired. My children wanted to turn back, but I kept them going. At last I began to wonder if I was expecting too much of them.

Finally we reached the top. It seemed like the top of the world. We could see for miles and miles. Everywhere we looked there was great beauty. We forgot all about our tired legs. As we stood there, my son put an arm around me and said, "Thanks, Dad, this is great!" His sister agreed.

David must have been thinking of something like that when he wrote, "He (God) makes my feet like the feet of a deer. And He sets me on my high places" (Psalm 18:33). Jesus said, "You will know the truth and the truth will make you free" (John 8:32). He was speaking not only of "freedom from" but of "freedom to." We are free from such things as disease and disappointment. We also are free to love and be loved. We are free to trust and to laugh.

Our study of young people who attend church shows the value of saving sex for marriage. The young people who were most unhappy with their lives were those who had had sex before marriage. They were more likely to say that they were lonely, angry or disappointed with life. They have no purpose in life. They do not trust other people.

You may say, "But the Test of Truth is based on God's Word. What if my young person does not believe the Bible? Will the Test of Truth and the Evidence of Truth help him?" Probably not. If a person does not believe the Bible, he will find it hard to use the Test of Truth and the Evidence of Truth. That is just what happens to many Christian young people when they go away to school. They cannot defend their faith and so they give up whatever belief they had when they went away.

When I was in school I thought Christianity was a joke. I set out to prove it wrong. After two years of careful study, I decided that it was not a joke. I trusted Christ as my Saviour. Since that time I have been writing and speaking on the evidences for the Christian faith. I wrote *Evidence That Demands a Verdict, More Evidence That Demands a Verdict* and *More than a Carpenter*. I wrote one book just for young people, *Don't Check Your Brains at the Door*.

You should consider getting some of those books. They will help you fully understand how to defend the Bible. But here I would like to give you a "quick defense" to use when you find any young person who doubts the Bible.

Do not disagree with the young person when he says the Bible may not be true. Instead ask him to examine the evidence.

71

Say, "If the Bible is true history, we should be able to test it in the same way we test any other history book." Then you can explain that there are three tests for history books. They are the bibliographical test, the internal evidence test and the external evidence test.

Any book written so many years ago comes to us only in copies. The bibliographical test tries to decide if the copy we have is the same as the writer wrote.

In the internal evidence test we try to see if the book agrees with itself. Here we look for two things. First, even if something seems to be wrong in the book we must accept it until it is proved to be wrong. Second, we must judge how right a writer is by how close he was to the things he was writing about. Was he in a position to know?

In the external evidence test we compare the writing with other material from the same time.

Remember that these are the tests that are used to check any history book. By these tests the Bible is more dependable than any other piece of writing from thousands of years ago.

We can believe the Bible. How we present the evidence for that belief, though, is all important. It can mean the difference between our young people accepting or rejecting the truth.

Chapter 8
Teaching the Truth

"I do not want to do this!" Gary Marsh told his wife as they stood outside the church. "You know I do not like this sort of thing."

Penny turned and smiled at Geena Santoro and Beth McConnell as they passed. Then she turned back to her husband. "We have to do something, Gary! What we have tried so far with Brittney has not worked." She stepped closer. "Look, I will tell the pastor you are having trouble with your voice. You will not have to say anything. Please?"

Gary was not happy about it, but he followed his wife into the church. They made their way into the pastor's office. There they found Pastor Milford and his wife with Geena, Beth and several others. As Gary and Penny sat down, Penny explained that Gary was having trouble with his voice.

The pastor began by telling about how he had been working with his son. He told how he had been showing his son a way for judging right from wrong based on the nature of God. Then he told of something he had thought of only a day or two before. Truth is not only true but helpful as well. That is, God protects us and provides for us when we obey His commands.

When he finished, everyone was silent. Diane Milford, the pastor's wife, finally said something. After she spoke the group began to discuss the ideas the pastor had talked about. They each told about how they were trying to help their own children.

"It seems so simple," Beth McConnell finally said. "I cannot believe that I never thought to talk about it with my sons."

"It is simple," the pastor said, "but it is not easy. I cannot begin to tell you how hard this whole thing has been for me. I never understood how careless I was about God's law. My children could not understand because I was saying one thing and doing another. I have failed to teach my children the commands of God. The Bible says we are to teach our children 'when you sit in your house and when you walk on the road and when you lie down and when you get up' (Deuteronomy 11:19). I confess to you that I have not done that. I have sinned. I have sinned as a man. I have sinned as a father."

No one spoke. Geena began to cry quietly. Then through her tears she began to tell about the failure of her marriage. She talked about how that had affected Melissa. "But I cannot believe it was wrong to leave Kenneth." She began to cry harder as the others remained silent. "There was just no other way," she continued. "It was like our marriage went down a certain path. After a while there was no turning back. There was just no other way!"

Beth put an arm around her friend and began to cry with her.

Geena turned to the pastor. "Maybe if I had known these things ten years ago it might have made a difference in my marriage. But I cannot save my marriage now. I cannot help Melissa save her marriage either."

DeVonne Davis rose from her chair and knelt before Geena. She also had raised a daughter alone. DeVonne looked into Geena's face and took her hand in her own. "You are right, Geena. Nothing the pastor said will change the past. Even if it could there is no way to be sure that our children would make better choices. But it is never too late to help our children. We can still help them see that choosing to live God's way is not only right but helpful, too."

Soon they were all on their knees, praying and crying. As the meeting ended they agreed to meet each week to report and to help one another.

Gary Marsh did not speak until he and Penny were alone in the car. Then he said, "Never make me do that again. You know I hate that sort of thing."

Penny was quiet for several minutes. Finally she said, "I am happy we went, though. I think the pastor was right. If we start doing some of those things with Brittney--"

"What?" he demanded. "Like telling her I am to blame for her sleeping with boys? Like I have been setting a bad example for her? I may not be the best father, but Brittney's problem is not that she has not been taught right from wrong. She knows. She just does not want to do what we tell her to do."

Penny spoke very quietly, "I just think–"

Gary would not let her finish. "I just think the pastor needs to deal with his son before he tries to tell me what to do with my daughter!"

Doing the Impossible

The idea of the Test of Truth and the Evidence of Truth may be simple. Accepting it and teaching it to a young person, though, may not be easy. At least it may not be easy at first. Every parent knows that talking with young people can be difficult. That is especially true if we are talking about something as hard to understand as absolute truth.

Not only is it very hard, but it is never finished. You just have to keep at it every day. That is what makes the job of being a parent so hard. But it is that day-after-day teaching that will plant the truth in our children.

God gave Israel the way for teaching our children. He said:
> Hear, O Israel! The Lord our God is one Lord! And you must love the Lord your God with all your heart and with all your soul and with all your strength. Keep these words

in your heart that I am telling you today. Do your best to teach them to your children. Talk about them when you sit in your house and when you walk on the road and when you lie down and when you get up. Tie them, as something special to see, on your hand and on your forehead. Write them beside the door of your house and on your gates (Deuteronomy 6:4-9).

God's way of teaching truth to young people demands a day-after-day effort. We are to teach when we sit, walk, lie down and rise up. That is, we are to teach all the time. In everything we do, we are to teach our children about God and His commands. Even in the most common parts of life, our children should see God in what we do.

The word "no" was probably one of the first words your child learned. Your very young child tried to take something you knew might hurt him. You removed his hand and said, "No!" He started to put his hand on something hot. You pulled his hand back and said, "No!" In each case you were teaching your child. You were pointing out the safe and acceptable action by giving a simple command. As the child grew older, you gave fuller commands. "Do not play with your food." "Do not go near the street."

Many parents never go beyond the commands, though. They never teach their children why the commands are important.

Following the pattern of Rule, to Basic Truth, to the Person of God Himself is very important. This is especially true in our relationships with our own children if we want them to understand what is right or wrong and why it is right or wrong.

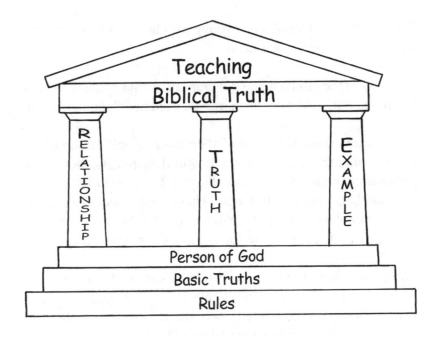

The Three Pillars

Imagine a large building. Three steps lead up to the door. The first step is Rule. The second step is Basic Truth. The third step is the Person of God Himself. Walk up those steps and enter the building. There you find that the roof is held up by three posts. The posts are relationship, example and truth.

Build a Relationship

The first post is relationship. We cannot teach truth until we have first developed a good relationship.

I once held a one-week conference at one of the largest churches in our country. In that week I had private talks with forty-two young people. The question they asked most often was, "What can I do about my father?" When I asked what they meant, they gave answers like:

> "He never has time for me."
> "He never talks to me."
> "He never does anything with me."

I asked all forty-two of those young people, "Can you talk with your father?" Only one said yes.

I also asked the girls, "If you got pregnant, could you talk to your father about it?" Most of them said they did not think they could.

In our study more than half of the young people from church families said that they do not talk with their fathers about their personal concerns. One in four said they hardly ever talked with their mothers about such things. These young people are more likely to think sex outside of marriage is all right. They are more likely to say that there is no such thing as absolute truth.

Young people who have a good relationship with their parents are different. They are more likely to feel satisfied with their lives. They are more likely to save sex for marriage. They are more likely to accept what the Bible says about how we should live. They are more likely to attend church and to read the Bible and pray every day.

It is no wonder that so many young people are failing to develop good ideas of right and wrong. They do not have the relationships with people who are able to teach them those things.

Truth is best understood within a relationship. For example, if I need to correct my children, I begin by asking a question that appeals to our relationship. I might ask, "Do you know that I love you?" By asking that question, I do not appeal to them on the basis of my power over them. I appeal to them on the basis of our relationship. If they answer yes to that question, I can be sure they will react well to my correction.

Some years ago my friend Dick Day and I wrote a book together. We called it *How to Be a Hero to Your Kids*. In it we examined the idea that "rules without a relationship lead to rebellion." Let me copy part of that book here. It makes very clear what I am talking about.

Dick and I have spoken to parents all over the world for the past fifteen years. Everywhere we go we find parents whose children are rebelling. The parents do not know what to do. It is easy to blame the society in which we live. We blame the television, movies and rock music.

We do not say that these things are not doing families real harm. In fact, many of the popular things in the world are real enemies to the life of the family. But fathers and mothers, please admit that the real problem is not with the world. The real problem is closer to home. It is right at our doors.

When parents make rules without first building relationships, the children will rebel. Sometimes the rebellion will be outward. Just as often it will be inward. Then the child may seem to be obeying the rules but is rebelling against them on the inside. That can lead to many problems.

We see the rules-without-relationships-lead-to-rebellion at work in every society. Once I spoke in the Philippines to more than six hundred pastors and church workers. After my talk more than two hundred of those men waited to talk with me. One pastor told me that his family had turned against him. His three children were "worse than any other young people in the church." They were all rebelling in one way or another. He asked me what he should do.

"Forget the rules," I told him.

"What?" he said. "That is what is wrong. They are not obeying any rules. They do not think they need to."

"I know what you are saying," I told him. "But I repeat, forget the rules. Take some of the ideas I talked about tonight and start building relationships. You have nothing to lose."

It is never too late to begin building relationships with your children. That is true even if they are no longer children. I remember one woman we talked with. She had four grown children. All four had rebelled against her. They caused her great pain and sorrow. We gave her the relationship-building ideas from *How to Be a Hero to Your Kids*. She went home and began the long, hard task of rebuilding those relationships. Five years later we met that woman again. She told us that her relationship with two of her children had turned around completely.

How do you test how good your relationship with a child or young person is? Try asking yourself:

> When is the last time you laughed together?
> When is the last time you cried together?
> Do you know what song he likes best?
> Do you know who she sits with in the school lunch room?
> When did she last seek your advice?
> When did you last break a promise to him?
> Do you more often ask questions of her or tell her what you think?
> Have you recently confessed a mistake to him?
> What do you know about her spiritual life?

The answers to such questions may show how good your relationship is. They may give you an idea about where to start to work to make the relationship better.

Be an Example

Several years ago I received a note from a man I did not know. He explained that he had come to my small town and waited around town until he saw me. Then he followed me around without me knowing it. He wanted to see if I live what I teach.

You are being watched, too. The way you live tells what you really believe about right and wrong.

Our study showed that thirty-five percent of our young people could not name even one person they thought was a good example. That is probably why so many young people have a hard time judging between right and wrong. They have no one to show them. They have no life to copy.

I have a friend named Frank. His son is called Frankie. Frank is a man of few words. Frankie is, too. Frank likes to stand with his hands in his pockets. Frankie stands in the same way. Frank is very good at fixing cars. Frankie loves cars. The father never spoke to his son about these things. The son simply copied his father.

If you want your children to follow the Bible's teaching, you must live that teaching before them. If you want them to accept absolute truth, you must let them see that you believe it yourself.

Young people do not like people who say one thing and do another. They believe there are many people like that. In fact, in our study seven out of ten young people said that there are many people like that in their church.

Our children often see when we are wrong. They rarely see us admit that failure and seek forgiveness. Only three out of ten of our young people say that their parents admit when they are wrong. We do not have to be perfect, but we do have to be honest and open. Our children should be able to see that we are really trying to live right.

I used to speak about every three years at a large church near Denver. Not long before one of my visits there the church got a new pastor. When one of the church leaders came to the airport to get me, I asked about the new pastor.

"Josh," he said, "it is so wonderful to have a pastor who loves his wife." He went on talking about the new pastor for most of an hour. He never talked about his preaching. All he talked about was the man's love for his wife. Finally he said, "I am more in love with my wife now than I have ever been." That pastor was living an important biblical truth before his people. He was teaching a truth by living it.

How can you be sure you are living the Bible's view of right and wrong before your young people? Try asking yourself:

What is there in my life that I do not want others to know?
How have I shown my belief in absolute truth this week?
Do I do things I tell my children not to do?
Am I willing to have others criticize my life?

Share the Truth

The effective teacher of right and wrong is the man or woman who is living right. The living must come before the teaching.

God told Moses, "Keep these words in your heart that I am telling you today. Do your best to teach them to your children" (Deuteronomy 6:6-7). The commands must be in your heart before you can teach them to your children.

As we said before, we must repeat the truth day after day. Sometimes we have to repeat it many times before the child fully understands and remembers it.

I remember asking my young daughter at the dinner table, "What did you learn in school today?"

"Nothing," she answered.

"You had to learn something," I urged.

"No," she said. "We just learned the same things we already knew."

I have since learned that that is the answer I can expect to that question. So much of teaching is going over the same material again and again. That is how we learn.

That is true of teaching about right and wrong as well. The Test of Truth and the Evidence of Truth must be taught to your children, not one or two times only, but many times. You must teach them every chance you get.

The following chapters will show how to use the Test of Truth and the Evidence of Truth to deal with different areas of life. Before we do that, though, we need to look at one more important point about teaching right from wrong. It is the most important point.

The Person of Truth

Pontius Pilate once asked, "What is truth?" (John 18:38). Jesus was standing before him at that very time. Earlier Jesus had told His disciples, "I am . . . the truth" (John 14:6). We cannot separate the idea of truth from the Person of Jesus Christ.

Knowing Jesus makes it possible for us to understand truth. It makes it possible for us to choose right over wrong. The person who knows Jesus knows the truth. He has the Truth living inside of him.

Jesus promised, "I will ask My Father and He will give you another Helper. He will be with you forever. He is the Spirit of Truth" (John 14:16-17). A little later He added, "The Holy Spirit is coming. He will lead you into all truth" (John 16:13). Without the Holy Spirit of Truth we cannot live pleasing to God.

We must teach our young people that when they accept Christ, the Holy Spirit enters their lives (Romans 8:9; 1 Corinthians 3:16). Obeying God's law does not make us Christians. Having the Holy Spirit in us does. That does not mean that obeying God's law is not important. It means that we obey because God's Holy Spirit is in us.

Here are the steps I have used to lead my own children into the Spirit-filled life.

1. Confess our sin (1 John 1:9). The Holy Spirit cannot fill and lead us when we choose to live apart from God. When we understand that we are not living in agreement with God's commands, we must admit that our own way is wrong. By faith we can claim God's love and forgiveness.

2. Trust God to fill us and lead us by His Spirit. Being filled with the Spirit means that He is directing our lives. It means that He is giving us His power to choose to do right (Romans 12:1-2; Ephesians 5:18; 1 John 5:14-15). To be filled with the Holy Spirit, we must give our all to God. We must ask the Holy Spirit to fill us. And we must believe that He does fill us.

3. Keep walking in the Spirit. We may still make mistakes or fall short. If we do we must turn back to God quickly and ask Him to forgive us. We must build our faith through reading the Bible and praying. We should not expect the world to help us live for God.

The greatest thing we can do for our young people is to lead them to the Person of Truth and the Spirit-filled life. They may still make mistakes, but they will be on the right path. They will be on the way to becoming "full-grown Christians standing as high and complete as Christ is Himself" (Ephesians 4:13).

Chapter 9

Coming to Terms With the Truth

Pastor James Milford came to the door of his son's bedroom and looked in. Philip was sitting on the floor at the end of the bed. He held a video game control in his hand. James looked from Philip to the screen where some small form was hurrying about. "What is this game called?" he asked as he sat on the floor beside his son.

Philip was slow to answer. "The Kingdom of Nobo," he finally said.

James acted as if he understood. He watched the screen for a while. Then he asked, "Can we talk for a minute?"

Philip did not take his eyes off the screen. James waited, watching his son. Philip finally looked at his father. "You want me to turn the game off?" he asked.

"Yes, please."

"Just let me save it." Philip gave some commands, and finally the screen went dark.

"I wondered if you might want to go do something, just the two of us," James said.

Philip looked at his father in surprise. "You mean now?"

"Do you have other plans?"

"No." Philip laid his head back against his bed. "I just do not feel like it."

James felt his anger rising, but he tried to control it. "Are you still mad at me?"

Philip only raised his shoulders and then let them fall back.

"Can I be honest?" James said. "I admit I am still a little mad at you. But I do not want to be. I have waited too long to say this." He waited a little before going on. "I am sorry, son. I am sorry for the way I raised my voice at you. I am sorry for some of the things I said."

Philip looked, not sure what his father meant, but said nothing.

"And I was wondering if you would do something for me. Will you help me control my anger? I really do not like it that I raise my voice at you and Sarah so much. When I start to raise my voice, will you remind me that we had this talk?"

The boy looked at his father for a long time. Finally, he raised his shoulders and let them fall again. "Whatever," he said.

James stood and walked to the doorway.

"Dad?"

James turned to face his son. Philip was still watching the dark screen. "Why can you not be this way all the time?"

The father thought about the question. After a long time, he asked, "What do you mean?"

"Why do you have to be so different around other people?"

"Different? What do you mean?"

"You turn into a preacher. It is like you act all different. And we have to act different, too. We have to put up a good show for the people at church."

"Now that is not true," James protested.

"It is, too." Anger was in Philip's voice. He stood to face his father. "We have to be the perfect family! But we are not! Tell the truth, Dad. When the school made me stay home for four days, were you mad because of what I did or because it made you look bad?"

James opened his mouth to speak but quickly closed it again.

"Tell the truth!" his son demanded again.

James wanted to argue with his son, to prove he was wrong. But as he looked into Philip's eyes, he saw that he already knew the truth. He stepped forward and stopped directly in front of Philip. He put a hand on each of his son's shoulders. "I am--I am sorry," he said.

Brittney Marsh went into the bathroom across from her bedroom. She quietly closed the door and locked it. Then she rested her head against the door for a minute before turning the light on. Carefully she pulled a small box from under her coat. She shook as she read the directions. She had to read them three or four times before she could understand them. Finally she began to do what they said.

When she finished, she sat and waited five minutes for the results. Her knees were shaking and there were tears in her eyes. She kept looking from her watch to the home pregnancy test and back again. Several times she was sure that something must be wrong with the test. Maybe she had not done it right. What if the test showed that she was pregnant? What would she do?

Geena Santoro hurried her friend Beth McConnell into the airport. "I am so afraid," she told Beth. "Why am I so afraid?"

"You will be fine," Beth said. "Whatever happens, you are doing the right thing. And do not worry about anything here. I will go to your house every other day to make sure everything is all right and to water your flowers for you."

"Thank you, Beth," Geena said. "What would I do without you?"

"Now, do not get your hopes up too high," Beth warned. "It would be nice if Melissa and Don got back together, but it probably is not going to happen."

"Oh, I know that. I know I cannot change the past. I will just be happy to do a little something about the future."

Tears were in Geena's eyes. She threw her arms around her friend before hurrying off to get on the airplane. Beth watched until Geena was out of sight.

———————————

Brittney was frightened when she heard her mother call to her. "Yes?" she answered through the bathroom door. Her heart was beating fast.

"Matt is on the telephone."

"Tell him I will call him back later."

"Are you all right? You have been in there a long time."

"Yes, I am fine. I will be out in a few minutes."

She listened to hear her mother leave. Then she again looked at the test lying on her knees. The results now showed that she was not pregnant. "Oh, thank You, Lord!" she cried quietly. "Thank You, God! Thank You! Thank You!"

She heard her mother pass by the door again and hurried into action. She put the test materials back into the box. Then she took everything out of the wastepaper can. Putting the box at the bottom of the wastepaper can, she put the other things on top of it.

She unlocked the door and opened it. No one was there. She hurried across to her room, closed the door and telephoned Matt.

Late that night Pastor Milford sat in his small office at home. His wife and children had gone to bed hours before. He sat without moving, thinking about his talk with Philip. *He is right*, he admitted. *I was mad because I knew there would be no way to keep Philip's actions a secret from the church. I was worried about what people would think.*

He lowered his head and prayed. "Oh, God, I was more concerned about me than I was about him. I was angry because he had sinned against me, not because he had sinned against You. Your heart was breaking for Philip. And I could not see how he had hurt You. I could not see how he had hurt himself. I was concerned only about how I could make things look good for the people of the church."

A new idea came to him. He stopped to think about it, turning it over in his mind. "Oh, Lord," he said. "I have been so foolish." He was remembering a time his family had returned from a trip. They got home earlier on a Sunday evening than they had expected. He told his family that they would put the car in the garage and leave the front of the house dark. That way no one would know that they were in town during the evening service.

He prayed for a long time with his head in his hands. It was not until after two o'clock in the morning that he began to write.

A crowd of about 175 people finished singing the song "Holy, Holy, Holy." They sat down and prepared to listen to the sermon by Pastor Milford.

"Two weeks ago, I stood before you and made a confession," he began. "I told you that I had failed as a father. I told you that our children do not accept our values. I said that we cannot blame the culture or the government. We cannot blame the schools or the media. The blame lies with parents like me who have failed to take charge of their children's training.

"God has not left me alone since that day. He has continued to speak to me gently but firmly and has led me to repentance." He looked at his notes as if he was not sure about how to continue. Then he raised his eyes to face the people.

"I have another confession to make this morning. I have not been completely honest with you. My family is not perfect--far from it. They are the people I love most in this world, but my children sometimes disobey me. I often disappoint them. You probably already knew that. But I have wanted so much to make myself and my family look good before God's people that I have not been fully honest with you. I have not lied. Neither have I told you the whole truth. I have been teaching my children to stop short of complete honesty as well.

"There are some things about me that you would think very wrong if you knew them." He began to tell about his talk with Philip. He told about how God had been dealing with him following that talk. "I have even told my children, 'Do not let anyone at church know about this.' I have asked them, 'What if your Sunday school teacher knew you acted this way?'

"I am not talking about sinful actions. I am talking about some choices my wife and I have made for our family. We have tried to hide those choices because we were afraid that God's people might not understand. 'My Christian brothers, this is not right!'

(James 3:10). Should a pastor keep things from his brothers and sisters in the church for fear that they will judge him too hard?

"Last night I began to understand that I have been telling my children one thing and teaching them something different by my actions. I have been trying to teach them to be honest. At the same time I have been involving them in my efforts to present a less-than-honest picture to the church. I have been trying to tell others that God is truth while I have been living a lie."

Many of the people would not look at the pastor as he talked. They looked at the floor or the walls. Some were looking at each other in disapproval.

"Last night I confessed all this to God and received His mercy. He brought the joy of His salvation back into my heart. I have made up my mind that from this day, with God's help, I will be honest and open before God and before you."

———————

Gary Marsh joined a small group of people outside the church after the service. Andy Porter was speaking as Gary arrived. "I had friends with me this morning. What are they going to think of our church now?"

"It just ruins the spirit of the service," Marjorie Henry said. "Services used to be so enjoyable here."

"Well, this morning just does it for me," Gary said. "I have no desire to come to this church again. If a man wants to get things off his conscience, fine--in the right place. But I come to church to hear the Word of the Lord, not the confessions of a man who cannot keep his son in line."

CHAPTER 10
What Is the Truth About Sex?

Brittney Marsh did not find her mother in the living room. So she climbed the stairs to the second floor. It was Saturday afternoon, and she had just arrived home from her high school ballgame. She hoped to borrow some money so that she could go shopping with friends.

She thought she heard Penny's voice coming from the bedroom. Her mother must be talking on the telephone, she thought. The bedroom door was not fully closed. So Brittney pushed on the door and stepped into the room.

Her mother was not on the telephone. Instead she sat on the edge of the bed drying her tears. A white bag lay at her feet. She tried to quiet her crying as she saw Brittney enter the room.

"Mother, what is wrong?" Brittney asked. She sat down beside her mother. "What is wrong?" she said again.

Penny turned then and looked at her oldest child. Her eyes were red from crying. She reached into the bag at her feet. "I found this when I was emptying the wastepaper this morning," she said. She pulled out the home pregnancy test Brittney had used last Saturday night.

Brittney was sorry she had not gotten the evidence out of the house. She opened her mouth to speak, but when she looked into her mother's face she could say nothing.

"Oh, Brittney," her mother said and broke into a new round of crying. Mother and daughter sat without speaking for what seemed like a long time. Finally Penny said, "I thought--I thought you said you always used protection."

"I do," Brittney answered quickly. "Well," she added, "almost always."

"Why did you not tell me?" Her voice was different now. She was more calm, like a mother inspecting a hurt on a child's head.

Brittney lowered her eyes and looked at the floor. "I do not know," she answered. Her voice shook. "I was just so afraid."

Penny put an arm around her daughter and pulled her close. After a little bit, she asked, "What did the test show? Are you pregnant?"

"No."

"Are you sure?"

"Yes."

Penny waited before she asked, "Remember how you felt when you thought you might be pregnant?"

"Yes. It was terrible. My hands would not stop shaking."

"Do you think that is what true love feels like?"

Brittney sat very still. "What do you mean?"

"Well, you were afraid. You felt alone. You had to go through that experience all by yourself. Are those the kinds of feelings you expect true love to produce?"

Brittney did not answer.

"See, Brittney, those are exactly the kinds of things God wants to protect you from. That is one of the reasons He tells us to 'flee sex sin.' He wants you and your husband to take a pregnancy test together, waiting hopefully for the result. He does not want you shaking in fear by yourself as you take it."

After another period of silence, she asked, "Does Matt know?"

Without taking her head from her mother's shoulder, Brittney answered that he did.

"How did he react to all this?"

"I am not sure. He is happy I am not pregnant, but he has not seemed the same lately."

"It might have frightened him, too."

"Yes, that is probably true." There was a sad note in Brittney's voice.

The Test of Truth

Have you ever watched as a painter painted a picture of a person? He sits the person five or ten feet away. Then as he paints he keeps looking at the person. Sometimes he will speak to the person. He may say, "Lift your head a little," or "turn your head this way." All the time he is painting he keeps looking at the person. The painter who does not do that will not produce a good likeness of the person.

The same is true when it comes to helping your children make good choices in the area of sex. In order to help them know what makes sex right, you must use the Test of Truth. This Test asks, How does it compare with the standard? We find the answer by looking at the Rules and Basic Truth, to the Person of God Himself. He is the One who made sex.

THE TEST OF TRUTH

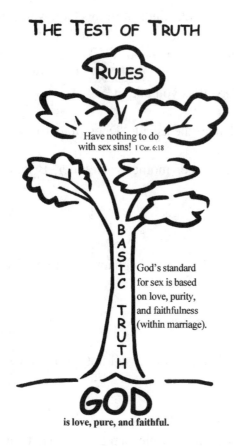

RULES

Have nothing to do with sex sins! 1 Cor. 6:18

BASIC TRUTH

God's standard for sex is based on love, purity, and faithfulness (within marriage).

GOD

is love, pure, and faithful.

Rule

In biblical terms, sex sin is always sex outside of marriage. God has made His rule clear: sex outside of marriage is wrong.

God has told us that many times. The people of Sodom and Gomorrah were destroyed because of their sin, which included sex sin. King David's sex sin with Bathsheba brought down the judgment of God. The Apostle Paul said that the death of twenty-three thousand Israelites was because of their sex sins (1 Corinthians 10:8). "These things show us something," the Bible says (1 Corinthians 10:6). They show us that "the Laws of the Lord are right" (Psalm 19:8).

Basic Truth

God's law against sex sin is not based on a desire to take away our freedom or to keep us from enjoying life. It is based on at least three important Basic Truths: love, purity and faithfulness.

The biblical standard for having sex is love. In a way our young people agree. In fact, 77 percent of our young people who have already had sex say that love would make them more likely to have sex. In the minds of our young people, love makes sex right. The problem is that our young people are working from a false idea of love.

Brittney Marsh believes that her love for Matt makes sex right. Because she loves him, she thinks it is right to express that love sexually. Her mistake is in accepting a wrong idea of love. True love, as defined by God, sets clear limits for sex. True love says that the happiness, health and spiritual growth of another person is as important to us as our own. Only that kind of love makes sex right.

Ephesians 5:28 helps us understand what the Bible means by "love." "So men should love their wives as they love their own bodies. He who loves his wife loves himself." What does it mean to love our own body as Scripture commands? The next verse explains: "For no man hates himself. He takes care of his own body. That is the way Christ does. He cares for His body which is the church."

The biblical standard of sex is one of purity. "Marriage should be respected by everyone. God will punish those who do sex sins and are not faithful in marriage" (Hebrews 13:4). God's standard for sex demands that the sexual relationship be kept pure and beautiful. God designed sex for three reasons: for having children (Genesis 1:28), for building spiritual oneness (Genesis 2:24) and for enjoyment (Proverbs 5:18-19). God planned that all of those would take place within marriage.

The biblical standard of sex is also one of faithfulness. Love and faithfulness go together. That is why marriage is at the center of biblical sexuality. It ties two people together for life. If the act of love is to produce the closeness God planned for it to produce, it must be faithful.

God's rules about human sexuality are based on love, purity and faithfulness. Those, in turn, are based on the Person of God Himself.

Person of God
God is love. "Those who do not love do not know God because God is love" (1 John 4:8). Love is not simply what God does. It is who He is. "Love believes all things. Love hopes for all things. Love keeps on in all things" (1 Corinthians 13:7).

God is pure. "The person who is looking for this (the return of Christ) to happen will keep himself pure because Christ is pure" (1 John 3:3). As the Prophet Habakkuk said, God's purity is such that His "eyes are too pure to look at sin" (Habakkuk 1:13).

God is faithful. "Know then that the Lord your God is God, the faithful God. He keeps His promise and shows His loving-kindness to those who love Him and keep His Laws, even to a thousand family groups (generations) in the future" (Deuteronomy 7:9). God cannot be unfaithful because faithfulness is not something He does. It is something He is.

Because God is pure, sex sin is offensive to Him. Because He is faithful, sex outside of marriage is offensive to Him. After King David sinned with Bathsheba, he was sorry. He confessed to God, "I have sinned against You, and You only" (Psalm 51:4). Was David forgetting that his sin had affected other people? No, he was simply confessing that his act was wrong because it went against who God is. It went against God's love, purity and faithfulness.

So then, the Test of Truth shows that the Bible's standard for sex is based on the nature of God. Brittney's relationship with Matt goes against God's nature. Their sexual relationship is not loving because they are not thinking about each other's happiness, health and spiritual growth as being as important as their own.

Their sexual relationship is not pure because it is not being enjoyed within marriage as God planned. It does not fit God's idea of faithfulness because it is done outside of a lifelong relationship. Brittney's sex with Matt is not wrong just because her parents say it is wrong. It is wrong because she goes against God's rule that sex is to be enjoyed within marriage.

We can say then that God's rules about sex are right for all people, for all times and for all places.

The Evidence of Truth

Some people will not accept what we have shown by the Test of Truth. That is true even of many of our church young people. Many parents think that young people will listen only to a warning about diseases that are passed from one person to another through sex. Most young people are more concerned about the fear of having a child. If we can show them the Evidence of Truth, young people will be more likely to accept the truth and reconsider their actions.

Brittney Marsh is like most young people. She thinks her mother's fear is about unprotected sex. But the thought of having a child frightens Brittney. With her mother's help, Brittney is beginning to understand that obeying God's rule about sex is for her good. It will provide for her greatest hopes and protect from her greatest fears. She's beginning to understand that good choices are not only right. They are also the best path to enjoyment and satisfaction because they protect and provide for her.

1. Protect from guilt and provide for spiritual blessings. God is the One who says what is right and what is wrong. When we go against His rule we feel guilty. Although Brittney said she did not feel guilty, she confessed that she sometimes felt "sad" after having sex. When she said that, she was describing guilt.

God's rule for sex provides for spiritual blessings. The blessing of a good conscience and a close walk with God cannot be measured. It is a wonderful thing to be able to come to your marriage knowing that you have saved yourself for your husband or wife.

2. Protect from an unplanned child and provide for a good atmosphere for raising a child. Every day in America 2,795 unmarried girls get pregnant and 1,106 of them have abortions. The girls who do not have abortions often face great difficulties. Many have to leave school. Many have serious health problems. Many feel left out of the things other young people do because they have to take care of a child.

Those girls who have abortions also have problems. Dr. Anne Catherine Speckard of the University of Minnesota reports the following long-term (five-to-ten years later) effects of abortion:

> 81 percent said they could not stop thinking about the aborted child
>
> 73 percent said they often thought about the abortion experience
>
> 54 percent said they had bad dreams about the abortion
>
> 72 percent said that they did not believe in God at the time of their abortion
>
> 96 percent said that they now believe abortion is murder.

God's rules for sex provide for a good atmosphere in which to raise a child. God's plan for every child is that it be loved and cared for by a man and a woman in a lifelong marriage. Studies show that is the best situation for raising a child.

3. Protect from disease and provide peace of mind. God's rules for sex protect from diseases that are passed along through having sex. Every day 4,219 young people in America catch such a disease. Among young people who obey God's rules about sex, there are no cases of those diseases. God's rules protect them.

God's rules for sex provide for peace of mind. I have never had to worry about diseases that come from having sex. Why? It is because I have followed God's rules of love, purity and faithfulness before marriage and in marriage.

4. Protect from fears about sex and provide for trust. God's rules for sex protect from fears about sex. God made sex so that it would give us an experience we would remember. As a result, wrong sex can produce effects that trouble us for a long time. It may make later sex within marriage less enjoyable and less satisfying.

God's rules for sex provide for trust. Sexual purity and faithfulness before marriage help to establish trust within marriage. That trust provides peace of mind for both husbands and wives when they are apart. Each knows that the other can be trusted. Why? It is because in the period before marriage, they proved what kind of persons they were.

That is why sex before marriage can be such a problem in a marriage. "He could not control himself before marriage," the wife reasons. "What makes me think he will control himself in marriage?" "She had other boys before she met me," the husband thinks. "What is to stop her from having others now?" In fact, there does seem to be good reason for such fears. A study of 100,000 women put it like this: "Sex before marriage . . . does not always lead to sex outside of marriage, but it does make it more likely."

5. Protect from emotional pain and provide for true closeness. God's rules for sex protect from emotional pain. The emotional costs of sex sin are very great. One young person explained the effects of her sex sin this way:

> Having sex before marriage was the most terrible experience of my life. It was not at all the satisfying experience the world made me believe it would be. . . . I know God has forgiven me, but I also know I can never make it as though it never happened. I do not look forward to the day when I have to tell the man I want to marry that he is not the only one. . . . I have given up my purity and I can never get it back again.

Another girl described her experience this way:

> After you have done it, you are really tied to that boy. It is as if he is your life. You feel really helpless. When the relationship ended, I felt really terrible. I cannot describe it. About a week after we had sex, we broke up because I found out he was going with other girls. It really hurt.

Those who obey God's rules are protected from the effects of sex sin.

God's rules about sex provide for true closeness. One woman wrote of the blessing of true closeness:

> Last July God gave me the most wonderful man in the world to be my husband. . . . He gave me someone I can share my deepest feelings with, someone I can talk to God with, someone I know will always love me and be faithful to me, someone I am glad I waited for.

> On our wedding night I experienced sex for the first time, and it was with my husband. I would not have wanted to share my first time with any other man. I had no wealth to offer my husband, but he did not ask for any. All he wanted was me, and that is just what I had to give him--all of me, untouched, his alone. That meant a great deal, and we both knew it.

God's rules for sex provide a degree of closeness that can be found only within marriage. God said, *"For this reason a man will leave his father and his mother, and will be joined to his wife. And they will become one flesh"* (Genesis 2:24).

God's rules for sex are meant to produce closeness. After all, God Himself said that "it is not good . . . to be alone" (Genesis 2:18). True love, purity and faithfulness are meant to result in a closeness of two people. When our lives agree with God's absolute truth, we can experience all the blessings of His protection and provision.

Putting Truth About Sex to Work

A battle is going on in our culture, and our young people are in danger. They need to hear the truth. They need to see the evidence for that truth. And they need help putting the truth to work in their lives "when [they] walk on the road and when [they] lie down and when [they] get up" (Deuteronomy. 6:7).

Parents, pastors and youth leaders can use many different ways to show how the truth works in a person's life. Here are some ideas on how to use what we have been discussing in this chapter with your children and young people.

Celebrate the anniversaries of your marriage.

Anniversaries are great times to let children know how faithfulness and purity have protected and provided for you in your marriage. Make your anniversary a family time. Tell your children what faithfulness in the marriage has done for your relationship. The more they see how your love, faithfulness and purity have blessed your lives and theirs, the greater effect it will have on them.

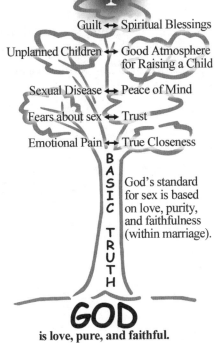

THE EVIDENCE OF TRUTH

PROTECTS FROM: PROVIDES FOR:

Guilt ↔ Spiritual Blessings

Unplanned Children ↔ Good Atmosphere for Raising a Child

Sexual Disease ↔ Peace of Mind

Fears about sex ↔ Trust

Emotional Pain ↔ True Closeness

BASIC TRUTH

God's standard for sex is based on love, purity, and faithfulness (within marriage).

GOD

is love, pure, and faithful.

THE EVIDENCE OF TRUTH IS ITS FRUIT.

Even younger children can understand the ideas of biblical love and faithfulness in marriage. You can explain your love for your wife by describing how she is as important to you as your own body. You can explain faithfulness in marriage by saying, "That is why I live only with your father (or mother)."

Go to weddings as a family. Make sure your children understand the importance of the wedding. Take time before and after the ceremony to talk about the promises the man and woman are making. Get a copy of the wedding ceremony and read it together with your younger children. Show how the marriage promises are based on the nature of God.

Use the media. Point out every false picture of love and sex you see or hear in the media. Talk about what is wrong and about how much better God's plan is. You may be surprised at how well your young people can use the Test of Truth and the Evidence of Truth.

By doing these things you will be preparing your children and young people to choose right over wrong. You will be helping them learn that God's rules for sex are right for all people, for all times and for all places.

CHAPTER 11

What Is the Truth About Honesty?

Philip Milford went down on his knees and laid the side of his face on the ground. He closed one eye, then opened it and closed the other. He raised his head and looked at the hole in the ground about five feet away.

"How long does it take to line up a shot?" his father asked.

Philip looked at his father. Then he got to his feet and stood over the ball. He drew back slowly, swung forward and gently hit the golf ball into the eighteenth hole.

"Yes!" Philip said as he raised his hand into the air. He smiled at his father. "That is a two."

Pastor Milford wrote down Philip's score and then began adding up their scores for the game.

"What is the score?" Philip asked when his father finished.

Pastor Milford acted unhappy as he handed the paper to his son. "I beat you!" the boy said. "Forty-nine to forty-one! I beat you bad!"

A smile broke across James Milford's face, and he put an arm around his son's neck.

"Yes, you did," he said. They both laughed. James tried to remember the last time he and Philip had laughed together.

Later that week Pastor Milford took Philip and his sister, Sarah, to Freez Whip for ice cream. He reached into his pocket for the money and pulled out a piece of paper with the money.

Philip took the paper from his father's hand and looked at it. "This is from our game!" He turned to his sister and showed her the paper. "See? I beat him bad."

Pastor Milford got an idea. "What if I told you that you did not really win that game?"

"But I did win!" Philip answered.

"What if I told you I put down false numbers to let you win?"

Philip's face changed. "No, you did not!"

"Would it make any difference if I had? You wanted to win."

"Yes, but…" The boy's face turned red. He was starting to get angry.

"Calm down, Philip. You won fairly. I did not let you win."

His son did not understand. Nine-year-old Sarah was watching and listening very carefully.

"Would it have made you unhappy if I had let you win?"

"Yes," Philip confessed. "I wanted to beat you."

"But you still would have won."

"It would not have been the same."

"Why not?"

Philip thought a little. "Because it would not have been real," he said finally. "It would not have meant anything."

"Right. Cheating would have robbed you of the satisfaction you got from winning. And you would not have been sure of yourself the next time we played."

106

They finished their ice cream and left the store. James stopped in front of the Freez Whip and looked at his daughter. "As I have told you before, honesty is right God is true. Honesty is part of His nature. But I also want you to understand that part of the reason God wants us to be honest is that He knows cheating is not fun. It robs us of many good things."

Our study shows that our young people fail in the area of honesty more than in most other areas. Two of every three of our young people say they have lied to a "parent, teacher or other adult" within the last three months. Six in ten say they have lied to another young person. About one in three admit that they have cheated on a test during that same time. And nearly one in six say they have recently stolen money or other things.

What has caused our children to be so dishonest? They have accepted man's idea of truth instead of God's. Our study shows that more than half of our youth believe that "lying is sometimes necessary."

Our young people have accepted the false in place of the true. They see lying as an easy way to get what they want. It makes them seem important to other young people. It is a way to gain the approval of their parents. They do not think it is wrong. They do not think about the bad things that come from it. They do not think about the good things that come from honesty. That is why they need to hear and understand the Test of Truth and the Evidence of Truth about honesty.

The Test of Truth

"Honesty is praised, and goes hungry," wrote Juvenal, a Roman writer of two thousand years ago. But why do most people praise honesty? What makes it right?

107

order to answer that we must ask, *How does it compare with the standard?* Remember, if we want to judge if something is right or wrong, we must follow it from the Rule, to Basic Truth, to the Person of God.

Rule

Thousands of years ago, God gave these commands to Moses: "Do not steal. Do not tell a lie about your neighbor" (Exodus 20:15-16). A little later God gave those commands again and made them a little fuller: "Do not steal. Be honest in what you do. Do not lie to one another. Do not lie when you make a promise in My name, and so put the name of your God to shame. I am the Lord. Do not make it hard for your neighbor or rob him" (Leviticus 19:11-13). God made it very clear to His people that it is wrong to lie, cheat and steal.

The Old Testament book of Joshua tells how the Lord's anger turned against Israel because Achan stole things when God destroyed Jericho. God said to Joshua, "They have stolen and lied. They have put them among their own things" (Joshua 7:11). God showed Joshua that Achan was the guilty one. Achan was killed. His home and family were destroyed.

More than a thousand years later, a husband and wife lied to the church. They wanted to make the church leaders think they were giving more than they were. The Apostle Peter said to Ananias (and later to his wife, Sapphira), "You have lied to God, not to men" (Acts 5:4). Ananias and Sapphira both fell down dead at Peter's feet.

The dishonesty of Achan was an offense to God because it went against His commands. Ananias and Sapphira sinned against God because they broke His law. But that is not the end of the story.

Basic Truth

God's commands against lying, stealing and cheating are based on a Basic Truth. That Basic Truth is honesty. It protects all who stay within its limits.

108

In many ways honesty is explained by what it will not do. An honest person will not lie. The Bible says, "So stop lying to each other. Tell the truth to your neighbor" (Ephesians 4:25). An honest person will not cheat. "Do not be fooled," Paul warned, ". . . those who always want to get more of everything . . . will have no place in the holy nation of God" (1 Corinthians 6:10). An honest person will not steal. It is the honest person's goal to "not steal . . . but prove they can be trusted in every way" (Titus 2:10).

The Basic Truth of honesty is not good in itself. It is good because it comes from the nature of God.

Person of God

When my daughter Kelly was in fourth grade, several students in her class took an object from the teacher's table while the teacher was out of the room. The children only wanted to play with the object, but it soon broke. They returned it to its place on the teacher's table. When the teacher found the damage, she asked one of the children what had happened. The girl knew that the others expected her to lie and so she did. Then the teacher asked Kelly, and she told the truth.

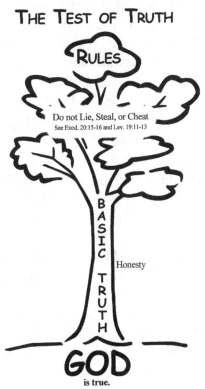

THE TEST OF TRUTH

RULES

Do not Lie, Steal, or Cheat
See Exod. 20:15-16 and Lev. 19:11-13

BASIC TRUTH

Honesty

GOD
is true.

The next day I talked with Kelly about what had happened. I told her she had done the right thing although the other students may blame her. "Kelly," I then asked, "why is lying wrong?"

"Because the Bible says it is wrong," she answered.

"Why does the Bible say it is wrong?"

"Because God commanded it."

"Why did God command it?"

She could not answer that. I took her hands in mine and looked into her eyes. "Because God is truth, Kelly. Truth comes from His nature, and whatever is against God's nature is sin."

Honesty is right because God is true. Truth is not something God does. It is a part of who He is. He is the God who "cannot lie" (Titus 1:2). Because God is true, lying and cheating are offenses against His nature. Because God is true, stealing is an insult to Him.

Honesty is good and right because God is true. That is objective and absolute. Dishonesty is evil and wrong because it is against God's nature. That also is objective and absolute. That is what makes dishonesty wrong for all people, for all times and for all places.

The Evidence of Truth

The Test of Truth will help Philip Milford understand that right and wrong are objective. That is, that decision is not ours to make. That comes from God. From that position, Philip's cheating and lying are wrong. But Philip also needs to examine the Evidence of Truth. That is what his father began to do with him in their talk at the ice-cream store.

Philip cheated because he had accepted several false ideas. He thought cheating was an easy way to do his schoolwork. He thought it would help him do better than his fellow students. He also thought it would make his father proud of him. When he was caught, he made his problem worse by trying to lie to his father. Again he saw lying as a way out of his problems. In each case Philip was wrong.

110

Philip is not alone in accepting false ideas. Our study shows that two out of three of our young people use dishonest means to get what they want. That is true even among youth who say they have a personal relationship with Jesus Christ.

James Milford has begun to help his children use the Evidence of Truth to examine questions of honesty. He is leading them in trying to find the answer to the question, *How does it agree with what is real?* He is searching with his son to see if dishonesty will do the things he thinks it will. He is trying to teach both Philip and Sarah that honesty shows God's nature. He is also working on his relationship with them and trying to be an example to them. He is helping them see that God's rule of honesty is not holding them back. In fact it can protect them and provide for them.

1. Protect from guilt and provide for a good conscience. Edgar Allan Poe's short story "The Telltale Heart" tells how a man killed another man. He buried the body under the floor of his room. But the crime was discovered when three policemen came to his room and questioned him. His guilt made him imagine he heard his victim's heart beating under the floor. In anger, he confessed and pointed the police to where the body was.

Guilt is one of the most powerful emotions. "My sins are gone over my head," David confessed. "Like a heavy load, they weigh too much for me" (Psalm 38:4). Guilt keeps the dishonest person from enjoying life to the fullest. The young person who obeys God's rule for honesty will be protected from guilt.

God's rules of honesty provide a clear conscience. David wrote, "O Lord, . . . Who may live on your holy hill? He who walks without blame and does what is right and good, and speaks the truth in his heart" (Psalm 15:1-2).

2. Protect from shame and provide for a sense of satisfaction. A habit of honesty can protect a person from the shame that results when his lying is discovered. After he was caught cheating,

Philip Milford refused to go back into the classroom. He was ashamed to face the looks of the other students.

God's rule of honesty provides a sense of satisfaction that the dishonest heart will never enjoy. Pastor Milford told his son, "Cheating would have robbed you of the satisfaction you got from winning." If Philip had not been caught cheating on his test, he may have shown his test paper to his father and gotten his praise. He could have taken no real satisfaction, though, because he had not earned it.

3. Protect from the habit of lying and provide a name for honesty. Every lie leads to more lies. In the end, the one who lies is trapped in his many lies and can find no way out.

Early in my relationship with my wife, Dottie, I told her, "I have something to say to you, and I do not need you to answer. I believe I am in love with you." She began laughing.

"You must not have heard me right," I said. "I said I think I am in love with you."

She pulled out a letter she had received from a woman who worked where I worked. The writer of the letter explained that she had heard that Dottie was going out with me. "Josh is known for going out with many women," the letter read. "So be very careful. I do not want you to be hurt." But the letter went on to say, "But one thing about Josh is that he will always be honest with you."

I have been thankful ever since that the writer of that letter thought of me as an honest man. That is one of the blessings of obeying God's rules of honesty. "A good name is to be chosen instead of many riches. Favor is better than silver and gold" (Proverbs 22:1).

4. Protect from ruined relationships and provide for trusting relationships. Several years ago, I had a series of meetings.

Ten to fifteen young people would agree to come and sit in a circle in the center of the room. Parents and other older people were permitted only to watch and listen. In one such meeting, a fifteen-year-old girl started crying. "I will never trust my mother again," she said.

I asked her why? She explained, "Two years ago I asked my mother if she and my father had waited until marriage to have sex, and she said 'yes.' The other day I learned that she had not waited. She lied to me. I will never trust her again."

God's rules of honesty provide for trust in relationships. Relationships are based on trust, and trust cannot continue in an atmosphere of lying. I tell my children, "If you tell the truth all the time, I can believe you all the time. But if you tell the truth only some of the time, I cannot believe you any of the time."

Putting the Truth About Honesty to Work

Many of the older people in America grew up on stories about Abraham Lincoln and George Washington. Those stories taught the value of honesty. Many of today's youth have never heard such stories. But we can still teach the value of honesty to today's youth.

Play the "what if" game. Ask young people to imagine how the world would be different if everyone in the world were completely honest. For example, we would not have to lock our

THE EVIDENCE OF TRUTH

PROTECTS FROM: PROVIDES FOR:

Guilt ↔ Good Conscience

Shame ↔ Sense of Satisfaction

The Habit of Lying ↔ A name for Honesty

Ruined ↔ Trusting Relationships   Relationships

BASIC TRUTH

Honesty.

GOD is true.

THE EVIDENCE OF TRUTH IS ITS FRUIT.

doors. Guide them from there into thinking about how honesty protects and provides for us. The next time your child locks a door, he or she will remember the value of honesty. Use times like that to remind them that when we are honest we honor God as a God of truth.

Use shopping trips to teach God's rules of honesty. Give younger children the money to pay for the things you buy. Take time to talk about the Test of Truth and the Evidence of Truth with them. Guide older youth in thinking about how stores must make up for people who steal by raising prices.

Give an "honesty gift." Make it a habit to say something nice when you see your children being honest. You may want to give them a small gift for their honesty.

Use the media to teach honesty. News reports often show the bad results of dishonesty and the blessings of honesty. Discuss such news stories with your children. In the same way, discuss things that happen at school or at work.

CHAPTER 12
What Is the Truth About Family?

Geena Santoro's daughter met her at the airport with a wide smile.

"Your hair!" Geena said, as they threw their arms around each other.

"Do you like it?" Melissa stepped back from her mother and raised a hand to her hair.

"It is so short!" Geena looked at her daughter, trying to get used to her short hair.

"I got so tired of my hair. I finally decided to cut it all off. Do you like it?"

"Well, you are so beautiful you would look good even if you had no hair," she said. Then she hurried on to add, "But do not get any ideas."

An hour later the two women sat in Melissa's house drinking tea. Geena looked around. There were no chairs in the small living room, only boxes. One room had a table and chairs, and the bedroom contained a bed and two or three other small pieces.

"I still have things to get from Don," Melissa explained. "I just have not had time to get them." Then with a big smile she announced, "I have a job."

"What about Don?"

The smile left Melissa's face. "What about Don?" she said.

Geena looked at her daughter and waited for her to continue.

"I think the owner is letting him stay in the house until he finds another place," Melissa finally answered. "Look, Mother, I know you do not like it, but we went through all this on the telephone, remember? Don and I just were not meant to be together."

"You married him, Melissa!"

"Like you married my father?"

Geena felt as if she had been hit in the face. A tense minute passed. Neither woman spoke. Finally, Melissa got up from the table and left the room.

Geena sat alone, her hands still holding the warm cup of tea. She shook her head. *I never could make her do what I wanted her to do*, she thought. *She always had a mind of her own. Once she made up her mind, there was just nothing anyone could do about it.* She smiled at her own helplessness.

She pushed her chair back from the table and followed her daughter into the bedroom. She found her sitting on the bed with her back against the wall. Geena stood by the only window and looked out. "I did not come here to argue with you," she said. *I never won an argument with you anyway*, she remembered. "I came because I wanted to be with you. I wanted to let you know how important you are to me."

She turned to face her daughter. "I have begun to understand that I am not responsible for you. It took God and a good friend to help me understand that I am responsible to you but not responsible for you. I want to be faithful to you. I want to show you a good example. I want to have a good relationship with you. I want to be here to help when you want my help."

Tears came into Melissa's eyes. "I really need to know that, Mother, and so does the baby."

116

Geena's eyes got wide and her mouth fell open.

Melissa smiled in answer to her mother's unspoken question. "Yes, I am pregnant. Due in December."

"Oh, a Christmas baby!" Geena said. She put her arms around her daughter and held her.

Later that day Geena asked, "Does Don know about the baby?"

Melissa set her coffee cup down on the table. "I told him yesterday," she said.

"Does that change anything?" Geena asked.

"It changes many things as far as money is concerned. But it does not mean we will be getting back together, if that is what you mean."

Melissa seemed to read her mother's face. "I know it is not going to be easy to take care of a child alone. But I have made up my mind to make a good home for my child."

"I know you will," Geena began. "But raising a child without a father — you know how hard it was not having your father around."

"Look, Mother, I am going to love my child and it is going to love me. We are going to be a great family with or without Don. People do it all the time these days. I am even thinking about having another single mother share my house. That will help with the load of being a single mother."

Melissa could see that her mother was not sure about that.

"Face it, Mother, it is not a perfect world. I am not going to run out and get a man just because my child may need a father."

117

Before Geena could say anything, Melissa hurried on, "How about going shopping? This place could use a few things."

"That sounds great," Geena said. She gathered the coffee cups and took them to the sink. "I want to be the first to get my grandchild some new clothes."

────────────

Geena Santoro is finding out that it is important to develop and keep a good relationship with her grown daughter. Melissa's ideas of marriage and family are already formed. But if Geena can learn new ideas about the family, perhaps her daughter can also.

Our young people are growing up in a culture that has tried to give a new meaning to marriage and family. Eighty percent of the children who were born right after World War II grew up in "intact" families. That is, they grew up in a home with both their birth father and their birth mother. Only 50 percent of the children born in the 1980s could expect to grow up in an intact family.

Like Melissa, the majority of church young people have accepted false ideas of marriage and family. Eight in ten say divorce is an acceptable way out of a marriage.

That is not to say that Melissa and her child will not be a family. Single-parent families are still families, but they are broken families. There are steps, though, that a single parent can take to limit or repair the damage divorce causes.

The Test of Truth

"Family values" were talked about during the 1992 election for president of the United States. During that election Newsweek magazine had a story that asked: "Whose values? Whose family? Who makes the choices?"

Those questions have already been answered. We can find those answers by the Test of Truth. In the Test of Truth we ask, *How does it compare to the standard?* Then we follow ideas from Rule, to Basic Truth, to the nature of God Himself.

Rule

In the first days of human life in the Garden of Eden, God made a wonderful plan for man. "It is not good for the man to be alone," He said. "I will make a helper that is right for him" (Genesis 2:18). So God made them male and female, a man and a woman, right for each other in every way.

One of the first rules God gave was, "For this reason a man will leave his father and his mother and will be joined to his wife. And they will become one flesh" (Genesis 2:24). Later Jesus said of marriage, "Let no man divide what God has put together" (Mark 10:9).

The Apostle Paul wrote, "I have this to say to those who are married. These words are from the Lord. A wife should not leave her husband. . . . The husband should not divorce his wife" (1 Corinthians 7:10-11). God gave many other commands about the family as well. Those commands show that God planned that our marriages and family relationships should be strong, loving and lasting relationships.

Basic Truth

Like all of God's rules, His commands about marriage and the family are based on a Basic Truth. That Basic Truth is oneness. God said, "A man will . . . be joined to his wife. And they will become one flesh" (Genesis 2:24). In the same way God planned that all the people in a family would be joined together.

God values oneness. The Bible says, "How good and how pleasing it is for brothers to live together as one" (Psalm 133:1). Jesus prayed that His disciples would "all be as one" (John 17:21). Paul told the Christians to "work hard to live together as one by the help of the Holy Spirit" (Ephesians 4:3).

THE TEST OF TRUTH

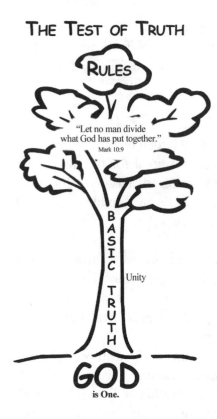

RULES

"Let no man divide
what God has put together."
Mark 10:9

BASIC TRUTH

Unity

GOD
is One.

Person of God

For hundreds of years faithful Jews have begun their daily prayers with the *shema*. The *shema* is given in Deuteronomy 6:4: "Hear, O Israel! The Lord our God is one Lord." It shows the oneness of God. In the New Testament, though, we learn that God is three Persons. For example, Jesus told His disciples to go and make disciples of all nations. Then He added, "Baptize them in the name of the Father and of the Son and of the Holy Spirit" (Matthew 28:19).

God is three Persons in One. He cannot be separated. Oneness is not something He tries for. It is not something He makes. It is something He is. Jesus said, "My Father and I are one" (John 10:30). "The Father is in me and I am in Him" (John 10:38). Oneness is part of God's nature. It is that oneness that He wants us to have in our marriages and in our families.

Because God is one, broken marriages and broken families are not like Him. Because God is one, His nature explains marriage and family as lasting for life. We can then say that oneness in marriage and family is right for all people, for all times and for all places.

The Evidence of Truth

God made marriage and the family not only to show His oneness, but also because He knew some things we did not. He wanted to protect and provide for us.

120

Our study shows that less than half of our young people want a marriage like that of their parents. Eight in ten see divorce as an answer to problems in a marriage. Less than half believe the family is an important part of American society.

At the same time, 90 percent of our young people believe that "God made marriage to last a lifetime." Most of our children, then, need to understand how the Evidence of Truth proves that God's rules for marriage and the family are right.

1. Protect from disappointment and provide for satisfaction. Disappointment always results from failure to obey God's rules for marriage and family. Our young people who live together outside of marriage are setting themselves up to be disappointed. That is true even if they plan to marry later.

One woman wrote:

> I wish I could tell every young person in America that you truly will get back what you plant. Living together may seem wonderful at first, but it makes more problems than you can imagine.
>
> I lived with my boyfriend for two years before we got married. I knew I was breaking my parents' hearts as well as my Heavenly Father's heart! My boyfriend was not a Christian, but I thought I could change him if we lived together.
>
> Before we married we lived with a "that-is-yours, this-is-mine" way of thinking. But that did not work once we got married. We had become too separate and too self-centered. It was nearly impossible for us to become "one flesh."

The writer of that letter thought of herself as a Christian when she moved in with her boyfriend. She thought she could lead him to Christ by living with him outside of marriage. Like too many of our children, she accepted the false (living together) for the real thing (marriage).

Many young people think of living together as a trial marriage. But a study shows that those who live together before marriage are 50 percent more likely to divorce after marriage. Also, a woman who lives with a man before marriage is far more likely to be beaten.

Most marriages experience some problems. But where the husband and the wife have "become one flesh" they can work through those problems together.

2. Protect from too-busy parents and provide for parents to be involved with their children. Parents sometimes get too busy to give their children the time they need. God planned for every child to have both a father and a mother. Two parents can make it possible for each parent to spend more time with the child. They can also give the child different ways of looking at problems.

Single parents find it impossible to do everything they need to do and have any time left for the children. There are not enough hours in the day for one parent to be both mother and father.

Parents who are divorced and remarried often find it even more difficult to have time with their children. They may see them only one day a week or for a month or two each year. Children of broken families suffer in many ways from this lack of their parents' time.

Remember that God's rules are like a cover of protection. When we move out from under that cover, we are no longer protected. We must help our young people understand the Evidence of Truth. Only then will they understand why marriage for life is in the best interests of both parents and children.

3. Protect from emotional problems and provide for emotional security. One study found that children in single-parent families are two or three times as likely to experience problems with their emotions. They are more likely to stop attending high school, to use drugs and to get in trouble with the law. Girls in single-parent families are more likely to have a child outside of marriage.

No one suffers more from a divorce than the children. The California Children of Divorce Study showed that children whose parents are divorced suffer emotionally for years after the divorce. God wants to protect our children from that emotional suffering. That is why He said, "Let no man divide what God has put together" (Mark 10:9).

God's rules for marriage and family provide for emotional security. Children need to know there are certain things they can always count on. They need that sense of security that says "God is in His heaven, all is right with the world."

4. Protect from problems in relationships and provide for good examples. Studies show that many children of broken marriages face severe problems in dealing with people. That is true not only while they are children but throughout their whole lives. Many find it difficult to become really close with any other person. It is hard for them to build long-lasting love relationships or to form a solid marriage. Some even find it hard to keep a job.

God's rules for marriage and family provide for good examples for children. When my daughter Kelly was much younger, I said to her, "Kelly, do you know that I love your mother?"

"Yes," she answered. "I know that."

"How do you know?"

"Because you always tell her."

"What if I lost my voice and could not tell her? How would you know then?"

"Because you always kiss her."

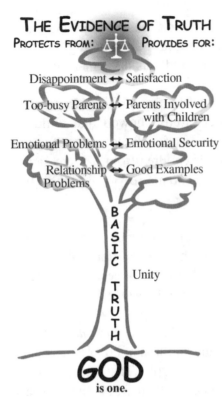

THE EVIDENCE OF TRUTH

PROTECTS FROM: ⚖ PROVIDES FOR:

Disappointment ↔ Satisfaction

Too-busy Parents ↔ Parents Involved with Children

Emotional Problems ↔ Emotional Security

Relationship Problems ↔ Good Examples

B
A
S
I
C

Unity

T
R
U
T
H

GOD
is one.

THE EVIDENCE OF TRUTH IS ITS FRUIT.

"What if I hurt my mouth and could not kiss her? Then how would you know?

Kelly thought about that. "Because of the way you treat her," she answered.

That is the answer I was looking for. It told me that I was setting a good example of a loving relationship between a man and a woman.

My children will be blessed for the rest of their lives by my wife's example of what a woman should be. She has given my daughters an example to follow and my son an example of what to look for in a woman.

Is There an Answer for Melissa?

Two-parent families are clearly better than single-parent families or second-marriage families.

We may be able to get an unmarried young person to accept that fact. But what about people in situations like Geena's or Melissa's? Are there any answers for these trying to raise children in a single-parent home?

There are steps a single parent can take. God said He was "a father to those who have no father. And He keeps the women safe whose husbands have died" (Psalm 68:5).

There is another living example of oneness that can provide some answers for those from broken families. That example is the church. The single parent who becomes involved in the local body of Christ can experience a living, healthy family. In some ways at least, that can make up for the loss of a husband or a wife. For the children it can make up in some ways for the loss of a father or a mother.

God wants each of us in the church to "be sad with those who are sad" (Romans 12:15). He wants us to "be happy with those who are happy." He wants us to "help each other in troubles and problems " (Galatians 6:2). That is the same kind of oneness we should experience in the family.

Are you a single parent? You and your child may have felt the emotional problems that often come from divorce or the death of a husband or a wife. Find a caring church and get involved. Get your child involved. Many broken families have found a great degree of healing as they have experienced the oneness the church provides.

Putting the Truth About Family to Work

Our children need to see the values of marriage and family. But how do we get our young people to put the truth to work in their lives?

Encourage your young people to become involved in the church youth group. A good youth group is an important part of a young person's life. That is true especially for a child from a single-parent home. Meet with your church youth worker to talk about your child's spiritual and emotional progress. Ask what you can do to help your child and the youth group.

Get involved in small-group meetings. Join a small group that is biblically based and that will help you as a parent. Some churches have single-parent small groups.

Pull out your wedding pictures. Use your wedding pictures to share what you believe about marriage. You may be surprised at how interested your children will be in the story of your wedding.

Talk about your children's births. At any age we are interested in hearing about the day we were born. Use that interest to provide your child a greater sense of belonging. Help your children understand that they came from your love for your husband or wife.

Show your love to your husband or wife. Let your children know how much you love your husband or wife. Be loving with each other around them. The more you show them how much you love your husband or wife, the more safe they will feel.

God's truth about marriage and family is absolute--it is for all people, for all times and for all places. Take the time to teach the Test of Truth and the Evidence of Truth about marriage and family to your children.

CHAPTER 13

What Is The Truth About Other Truths?

Pastor James Milford opened his front door. Penny Marsh stood alone on the step. "Come in, Penny," he said. Many others were already there. Most were sitting on chairs, but some were sitting on the floor. Geena Santoro stood in the opening between the living room and another room. The pastor closed the door and turned toward the crowd.

"I did not think about how large this group had grown when I invited you to meet here this evening," he said. The number of people attending the church had gone down since the pastor had confessed his family problems several months before. But this group had grown from eight to between twenty and thirty parents.

"I want to thank you all for agreeing to meet here today," he continued. "I explained the reason to some of you on the telephone. Just yesterday we moved my father-in-law out of the nursing home and into our extra bedroom. Diane did not want to leave him just yet, but she did not want to miss this meeting either.

"We decided we could best be responsible for him by having him in our home. We think it will be better for us as well as for him. He is weak in body, but strong in faith. He may be able to help our family stand against the culture better than we have been doing."

He asked if any wished to share their experiences of the past week. Geena Santora spoke up. "I just got back from visiting Melissa. I never thought I would get so tired of talking, but I am very happy I went. I even had lunch with Don." She went on to tell the details of her visit with Melissa.

"I doubt if they will ever get back together again," she finished, "but I feel better about Melissa. And we found a wonderful little church that might help her through it all. They even have a small group for single parents, so I am pleased about that. I would like to ask for prayer that she and the baby will be able to experience God's oneness in the future better than she has in the past."

Several in the group closed their eyes as DeVonne Davis began praying. When she finished, Doug Withers began praying. By the time the people in the crowded room raised their heads and opened their eyes, the room seemed to be alive with the Spirit of God.

Pastor Milford, sitting on the floor by the front door, waited for a little before speaking. He drew a deep breath. "Philip and I have come a long way in our relationship. Little by little he is opening up to me and beginning to trust me. And Diane and I have been trying to use every chance we get to talk with him about the Test of Truth and the Evidence of Truth."

Someone asked how Philip was progressing.

"He understands up here," the pastor said, pointing to his head. "He can use the Test of Truth and the Evidence of Truth almost as well as I can. That is a big change from a month or two ago. But I am still waiting for him to show that he is willing to make the right choices."

"Sometimes our children choose to go their own way," Beth McConnell said.

"I have some really good news to report." Every head in the room turned toward Penny Marsh. "I have been trying really hard to help Brittney, but I have had to do it mostly alone. Gary is really having a hard time with what we are doing. Anyway, some things have happened recently that have really helped Brittney see that God's rules are for her good.

"We were up until three one night talking about her relationships and what she wants and what God wants for her. To make a long story short, she broke up with her boyfriend this week. She said she wants to wait for God's best for her! In a way, I am so happy we have gone through this with Brittney. Now I will be able to really help Lauren and Michael as they get older. I have not been this hopeful about my children in years."

Diane Milford put an arm around Penny's shoulder and pulled her close.

One of the group began to pray again, a prayer of praise for what God was doing in and through each person in the room. That first prayer was followed by several others. The prayers were mixed with tears and songs of praise. Many minutes passed and still the praying continued. No one was in a hurry to stop. Every mind in the room was caught up in the Spirit of God.

When the praying and singing stopped, the group waited in silence. Everyone seemed to sense the nearness of God. Finally, Geena Santoro spoke.

"God, I want to thank You for what all this has done for me." She had tears in her eyes but her voice did not shake. "It has given me a new sense of You. It has helped me understand that everything comes from You. I see now how far I had gotten away from You. I see how much I need You. I need Your purity. I need Your holiness. I need Your faithfulness. I need You." She stopped and then said again, "I need You!"

———————————

Geena and the others have been using the Test of Truth and the Evidence of Truth to discover the values of sexual purity, honesty and family. They have begun to go beyond those to discover the truth in other areas as well.

In this chapter we will look at five of those other areas. We will not deal with these as fully as we have treated the values of sexual purity, honesty and family.

What Is the Truth About Love?

It has been said that love is the language all the world knows. Everyone praises love as the greatest value. But why? Why is love a value at all?

The Test of Truth About Love

Rule

A Jewish teacher once asked Jesus a question that many teachers before him had discussed. "'Teacher, which one is the greatest of the Laws?' Jesus said to him, 'You must love the Lord your God with all your heart and with all your soul and with all your mind.' This is the first and greatest of the Laws. The second is like it, 'You must love your neighbor as you love yourself'" (Matthew 22:37-39).

The greatest rule in the law, then, is to love. Jesus even went so far as to say, "Love those who hate you. . . . Pray for those who do bad things to you. . . . Then you may be sons of your Father Who is in heaven" (Matthew 5:44-45). The rule is clear: love for everyone is commanded.

Basic Truth

Like all rules, these commands point to a Basic Truth: love for God and love for others. The Basic Truth is larger than the rule. We might make some excuse for not obeying the command in some cases, but we cannot deny the Basic Truth.

Person of God

In the end, love is not right just because it is commanded. It is not right just because it is a Basic Truth. It is right because God
130

is like that. The rule and the Basic Truth both point to the Person of God Himself. "God is love" (1 John 4:16). He loves us so much that while we were still His enemies Christ died for us (Romans 5:8). But love is not something He does. It is something He is.

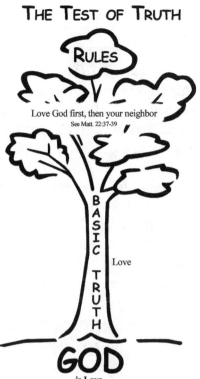

THE TEST OF TRUTH

RULES

Love God first, then your neighbor
See Matt. 22:37-39

BASIC TRUTH

Love

GOD
is Love.

We can say then that love for God and love for others is right for all people, for all times and for all places.

The Evidence of Truth About Love

Few people would argue with the idea that love is a good thing. Yet many have hate in their hearts. They may even believe they have a good reason to hate. But the Evidence of Truth is nowhere more clear than in this area.

1. Protect from fighting and provide for peace. I grew up hating my father. Everyone in our town knew about my father's drinking. When my friends joked about him, I laughed. I hoped my laughing would hide my pain. Hate for my father filled my life and robbed me of peace. Not long after I became a Christian, though, I began to love my father. I helped him trust Christ for salvation. Fourteen months later he died, but I had learned what love can do. Fourteen months of loving my father did more for me than twenty years of hating him had ever done.

2. Protect from self-centeredness and provide for satisfaction. I know a woman who judges everything that happens in her life by how it affects her. Though she has some friends, she has not really learned to love any of them. She loves only herself, and it shows.

The person who loves God and others shows interest in the ideas and interests of others. He often enjoys giving as much as receiving and finds joy in sharing with others and caring for them. Such a person is usually better liked and more successful than the self-centered person.

3. Protect from spiritual emptiness and provide for spiritual blessing. The Apostle John wrote, "The person who does not love has not passed from death into life. A man who hates his brother is a killer in his heart. You know that life which lasts forever is not in one who kills" (1 John 3:14-15). Such strong language shows the tragic spiritual results God wants to protect us from.

THE EVIDENCE OF TRUTH

PROTECTS FROM: PROVIDES FOR:

Fighting ↔ Peace

Self-centeredness ↔ Satisfaction

Spiritual Emptiness ↔ Spiritual Blessings

BASIC TRUTH

Love

GOD
is love.

THE EVIDENCE OF TRUTH IS ITS FRUIT.

Putting the Truth About Love to Work

Like any other value, love must be taught. Its value must be followed back to the nature of God by using the Test of Truth. Its good must be shown through the Evidence of Truth. There are many ways to do this.

Show love for God in your family. Before your younger children leave for school, ask them, "How can we show our love for God today?" Remind your young people sometimes that the offering in church is one way you show love for God.

132

Show love for one another in your home. Young people learn what love should look like from their family. Point out to your children the ways you show your love for them or for others.

Teach your children to love. Learn to say such things as, "You remind me of God when you show love to your brother" or "The way you treated Mrs. Sparks made me think of God's love."

What Is the Truth About Fairness?

How do you react when another person pushes in front of you in line? How do you feel when another person takes credit for your ideas at work? If you are like most people, you react by saying, "That is not fair!"

The Test of Truth About Fairness

Rule

The Bible has many rules such as, "Do the right thing for the weak and those without a father. Stand up for the rights of those who are suffering and in need" (Psalm 82:3). All these rules are included in what has been called "the Golden Rule": "Do for other people what you would like to have them do for you" (Luke 6:31).

Basic Truth

Fairness is the Basic Truth behind all the rules about how we should treat other people. God told the ancient Israelite judges, "Follow what is right, and only what is right. Then you will live and receive the land the Lord your God is giving you" (Deuteronomy 16:20).

Person of God

Fairness is not good just because God commands it. It is good because it is based on the Person of God Himself. Fairness is not something God does. It is something He is. He is a fair God. God "does what is right," Paul wrote (2 Thessalonians 1:6). He is "the Rock," Moses sang. "His work is perfect. All His ways are right and fair" (Deuteronomy 32:4). We should be fair because

133

THE TEST OF TRUTH

RULES

"Do for other people what you would
like to have them do for you."
Luke 6:31

BASIC TRUTH

Fairness

GOD
is Fair.

God is fair. The Test of Truth shows that fairness is based on the nature of our just God. We can say then that fairness is right for all people, for all times and for all places.

The Evidence of Truth About Fairness

Fairness is shown to be right because it is like the nature of God Himself. The Evidence of Truth confirms the Test of Truth.

1. Protect from a desire to punish and provide for a clear conscience. In Moses' day, an unfairness done by one person would often make trouble for his whole family. God's rules were made to protect His people from such results. The man or woman who treats other people fairly will often save himself from much trouble.

2. Protect from guilt and provide for peace.
I once knew a man who had treated another worker unfairly. The unfair man got along well in his work and continued to gain power and influence. The other worker worked hard, too, but no one ever praised him for it. But the unfair man was troubled by his own unfairness. He did not like to be around the man he had wronged. When he had to be near him, he would not look at him. That man was troubled by guilt and shame for what he did. The other man worked quietly and happily until he retired.

While unfairness always hurts the victim, it also often hurts far worse the one who does it. Those who obey God's rules about fairness enjoy a clear conscience toward others.

134

3. Protect from dishonor and provide honor. A name for fairness brings honor. My wife was once elected by her group as the one who would serve in a situation that demanded honesty. Everyone agreed that she should be chosen because "she has never treated any of us unfairly." People value a just man or woman. Fairness pleases God Himself, "For the Lord loves what is fair and right" (Psalm 37:28).

Putting the Truth About Fairness to Work

Parents, pastors, teachers and youth workers have many chances every day to teach fairness to their young people.

Be an example of fairness. Treat each child fairly. That does not mean you always treat them exactly the same. But help them understand how treatment that is "different" can still be fair. Demand that they treat their brothers, sisters and friends fairly.

Take every chance you get to point out that everyone wants to be treated fairly. Help them understand that fairness is objective and absolute. It is right for all people, for all times and for all places.

Help children understand how simple things such as taking turns or sharing play things show God's nature. They help us treat other people fairly.

Use news of court trials and government actions to talk with your older children and explore their

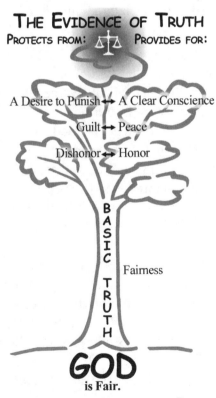

THE EVIDENCE OF TRUTH

PROTECTS FROM: PROVIDES FOR:

A Desire to Punish ↔ A Clear Conscience

Guilt ↔ Peace

Dishonor ↔ Honor

BASIC

Fairness

TRUTH

GOD
is Fair.

THE EVIDENCE OF TRUTH IS ITS FRUIT.

135

ideas of fairness. Remember to use the Test of Truth and the Evidence of Truth to explain the value of fairness.

Be open and reasonable when your child says your family rules are not fair. Use such times to discuss the fairness or unfairness of family rules. What might happen if the rule were canceled? Use the Test of Truth to help your children see why fairness is right. Use the Evidence of Truth to help them see what good can come from fairness.

What Is the Truth About Mercy?

"The good of mercy is not worn out," Portia told Shylock in Shakespeare's play *The Merchant of Venice*. "It falls as the gentle rain from heaven upon the place below." Many people and cultures agree that mercy is a good thing. It is like gentle rain from heaven. But why is it right to be merciful? What makes mercy a good thing?

The Test of Truth About Mercy

Rule

The Prophet Micah warned the people of his day that their empty worship did not fool either God or man. "O man, He has told you what is good. What does the Lord ask of you but to do what is fair and to love kindness, and to walk without pride with your God?" (Micah 6:8). Micah reduced God's law down to three simple rules. The command to "love kindness," or mercy, was one of them. Micah saw his people's failure to obey those rules as a sure road to punishment.

The Prophet Isaiah said, "Share your food with the hungry, and bring the poor man into your house who has no home of his own. . . . give clothes to the person you see who has no clothes" (Isaiah 58:7). The writer of Hebrews told the Christians to "remember those in prison. Think of them as if you were in prison with them. Remember those who are suffering because of what others have done to them" (Hebrews 13:3).

Basic Truth

Such rules are based on the Basic Truth of mercy. The rules show that God values mercy.

Person of God

The rule to "love mercy" is not right because it is based on a Basic Truth. It is right because it comes from God as One who "is happy to show loving-kindness" (Micah 7:18). The mercy of God was best shown to us in Jesus Christ. He accepted the Samaritan woman. He freed the daughter of a Canaanite woman from an evil spirit. He healed the sick. He spoke blessing to the woman caught in sex sin. He forgave those who put Him on the cross. He died so that we might escape the punishment for our sins.

We can say then that showing mercy is right for all people, for all times and for all places.

The Evidence of Truth About Mercy

The Test of Truth shows that mercy is based on the nature of God Himself. The Evidence of Truth shows that mercy is not only right, but it also produces good results.

1. Protect from want and provide for blessing. Mercy blesses both the person who receives mercy and the person who shows mercy. The person who will not show mercy must carry the shame of a mean spirit. The person who shows mercy enjoys the good feeling mercy gives.

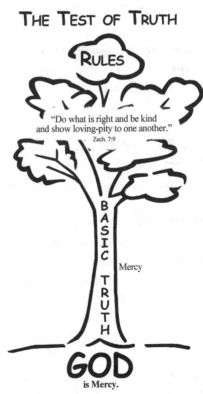

THE TEST OF TRUTH

RULES

"Do what is right and be kind and show loving-pity to one another."
Zech. 7:9

BASIC TRUTH

Mercy

GOD
is Mercy.

137

2. Protect from punishment and provide for kind treatment. Jesus said, "Give, and it will be given to you. You will have more than enough. It can be pushed down and shaken together and it will still run over as it is given to you" (Luke 6:38). The person who shows mercy will receive mercy. He will receive mercy not only from God but from others as well. But the person who will not show mercy will not receive mercy from either God or others.

3. Protect from unforgiveness and provide for forgiveness. Jesus said, "If you forgive people their sins, your Father in heaven will forgive your sins, also. If you do not forgive people their sins, your Father will not forgive your sins" (Matthew 6:14-15). That is very clear.

Putting the Truth About Mercy to Work

We can help form the biblical value of mercy in our children by teaching the Test of Truth and the Evidence of Truth.

Show mercy. Go out of your way to help others. Find things to do that will help a young person experience the blessings of showing mercy to others.

Discuss with older young people how Christ's atonement satisfied God's mercy. Use that example as a way to teach that fairness and mercy can go together. Ask, "How can we be both fair and merciful with each other?"

When you must correct your children, teach mercy by making the punishment less if they will try to make up for their sin. For example, you might say, "Susie, you took your brother's radio without asking. Then because you were careless, you lost it. What you have done is unfair to your brother. But if you will apologize to your brother and buy him a new radio, I will consider the incident closed."

When a child is having a hard time forgiving another, explain the value of mercy and what happens when we do

not forgive. Help him understand that unless he is willing to forgive others he will not be able to receive forgiveness for himself.

Ask your young person which he would choose to receive, fairness or mercy. Ask him to explain why. Ask which he would choose to give, fairness or mercy. Ask him to explain that answer as well.

What Is the Truth About Respect?

Everyone wants to be respected. But many of us are not good at showing respect for others. That is especially true of our young people.

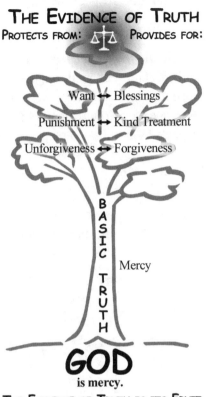

THE EVIDENCE OF TRUTH

PROTECTS FROM: PROVIDES FOR:

Want ↔ Blessings

Punishment ↔ Kind Treatment

Unforgiveness ↔ Forgiveness

BASIC TRUTH

Mercy

GOD
is mercy.

THE EVIDENCE OF TRUTH IS ITS FRUIT.

The Test of Truth About Respect

Rule

The Bible says that the first command with promise is, "Respect your father and your mother" (Ephesians 6:2). The Word of God has many similar rules. We are told to honor the king "because he is your Lord" (Psalm 45:11). We are told to "honor an older person and you will honor your God" (Leviticus 19:32). The Bible also gives rules about how husbands and wives, children and parents, masters and slaves are to honor one another.

Basic Truth

The Basic Truth behind all those rules is respect. The Bible makes it clear that we should "show respect to all men" (1 Peter 2:17). It often seems that children do not respect their parents.

139

Men do not respect women. Students do not respect their teachers. Christians do not respect their church leaders.

We should show respect for all people but especially for our leaders. God has made many leaders that we are commanded to respect. These include government officers, parents, teachers and church leaders (see Romans 13:1-7 for example). The person who respects God will also respect those He allows to be leaders.

Person of God

Respecting others is right because there is something about each of us that comes from the very nature of God Himself. God is Spirit and in Him is life (John 4:24; John 1:4). It is that part of His nature that every human being shares with Him. God "breathed into his nose the breath of life. Man became a living being" (Genesis 2:7). Every person should be respected because he or she is made in the likeness of God.

THE TEST OF TRUTH

Show respect for each other and the leaders of the land.
Romans 12:10 and Romans 13:1

Also, when we respect and obey our leaders, we honor God as Leader over all. "There is no power given but from God, and all leaders are allowed by God" (Romans 13:1). We can say then that showing respect for others and for our leaders is right for all people, for all times and for all places.

140

The Evidence of Truth About Respect

The Test of Truth shows us that respect for others and for our leaders is right because it is based on the nature of God. The Evidence of Truth shows us how respect works in real life.

THE EVIDENCE OF TRUTH

PROTECTS FROM: PROVIDES FOR:

Self-Criticism ↔ Self-Worth

Harmful ↔ Healthy
Relationships   Relationships

Offense ↔ A Pleasing Nature

Punishment ↔ Praise

BASIC TRUTH

Respect

GOD
is life and above all.
THE EVIDENCE OF TRUTH IS ITS FRUIT.

1. Protect from self-criticism and provide for self-worth. Respect for all people reminds me that I, too, am made in the likeness of God. As I treat others with respect, I remind myself that I have worth. This is not a permit for sinful pride. It is in obedience to the biblical command. "I ask each one of you not to think more of himself than he should think. Instead, think in the right way toward yourself by the faith God has given you" (Romans 12:3). We are not to think more highly of ourselves than what we really are or less than we really are.

2. Protect from harmful relationships and provide for healthy relationships. Respect for others makes a solid base for relationships. It creates an atmosphere of trust and love.

3. Protect from offense and provide for a pleasing nature. Several years ago I met a fifteen-year-old boy I will call Brett. He was easy to like until I saw how he treated his mother. He did not treat her with respect. He called her names and said things to hurt her. I told him that his treatment of her was offensive. God's rule of respect

141

for others protects from that kind of offense. On the other hand, people like to be around a person who shows respect for others.

4. Protect from punishment and provide for praise. Remember that God's rule of respect also includes respect for those who are leaders. The leaders we have are allowed by God. And God's Word says, "The person who does not obey the leaders of the land is working against what God has done. Anyone who does that will be punished" (Romans 13:2).

When we fail to honor leaders we suffer punishment. When we respect our leaders we live free of fear of punishment and enjoy the praise of those leaders. "Do you want to be free from fear of them? Then do what is right. You will be respected instead" (Romans 13:3).

Putting the Truth About Respect to Work

How do we help our young people develop the value of respect? How do we get them to respect themselves, others and leaders?

As in other areas, example is the most powerful teaching tool for teaching respect. What kind of example are you? How do you treat your own father and mother? How do you speak to your young people about others? How do you show respect for your husband or wife? How do you show respect for leaders in the church?

Treat young people with respect. They also are made in the likeness of God. Ask what they think, and listen when they answer.

Congratulate children when you see or hear them showing respect. Explain to them why you value their actions.

Teach your children how to show respect for people. Explain such things as opening the door for someone.

What Is the Truth About Self-Control?

Isaac Bashevis Singer said, "Man cannot live without self-control." Yet many people do just that.

The Test of Truth About Self-Control

Rule

God has commanded self-control. Jesus said that "anyone who even looks at a woman with a sinful desire" is guilty of sex sin (Matthew 5:28). Christians should not use "foolish talk" (Ephesians 5:4). They should not become angry (Colossians 3:8). They should not get drunk (Ephesians 5:18).

Basic Truth

The Basic Truth behind all these rules is that of self-control. God wants us to control our desires instead of being controlled by them. We can do that only through the power of His Spirit.

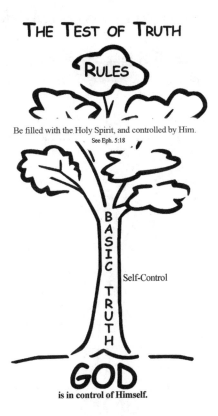

THE TEST OF TRUTH

RULES

Be filled with the Holy Spirit, and controlled by Him.
See Eph. 5:18

BASIC TRUTH

Self-Control

GOD
is in control of Himself.

Person of God

The reason self-control is a good thing is that God is like that Himself. He delays His anger. The Bible says, "The Lord is slow to anger" (Numbers. 14:18). God was not quick to punish the Israelites after they left Egypt although they did many things that displeased Him. "Yet I looked on them with pity and did not destroy them. I did not make an end of them in the desert" (Ezekiel 20:17).

Jesus was the best example of self-control when He stood before the Roman and Jewish officials and "did not say a word" (Mark 15:5). When we show self-control, we act like God. We can say then that self-control is right for all people, for all times and for all places.

The Evidence of Truth About Self-Control

THE EVIDENCE OF TRUTH
PROTECTS FROM: PROVIDES FOR:

Sorrow ↔ Enjoyment
Shame ↔ Respect

B
A
S
I
C

Self-Control

T
R
U
T
H

GOD
is in control of Himself.
THE EVIDENCE OF TRUTH IS ITS FRUIT.

We can help our young people see not only that self-control is right, but that it also is wise.

1. Protect from sorrow and provide for enjoyment. Dr. S.I. McMillen, author of *None of These Diseases,* tells of this experience:

I remember a certain New Year's Day. My wife and I got up feeling fresh and happy. We enjoyed a good breakfast. At noon we enjoyed a fine New Year's dinner. But that was not true of the other two husbands and wives who visited us. They had seen the New Year in by getting drunk and had spent the whole morning fighting sickness.

Self-control can make many things in life more enjoyable. A strong person may bring many areas of his life into control. But if we are to live pleasing to God in every area of our lives, we must lead a Spirit-filled life.

2. *Protect from shame and provide for respect.* I know an intelligent man who is a good leader. He once enjoyed the respect of many who worked for him. But any time this man gets drunk he acts like a fool. His lack of self-control ruins his workers' respect for him and limits his value to the company. The self-controlled person, on the other hand, often gains the respect of others who see self-control as a good thing.

Putting the Truth About Self-Control to Work

The Test of Truth bases self-control on the nature of God. The Evidence of Truth shows its blessings. All who want to influence young people must be open to every chance to use the Test of Truth and the Evidence of Truth to teach self-control.

Be open and honest about your own efforts to develop self-control. Ask others to help you become more self-controlled.

Take every chance you see to help young people understand that God is a God who is self-controlled. Explore with them examples of God's self-control from the Bible.

Praise young people when they show self-control. Praise a child who controls his anger on the playground. Praise a young person who uses money wisely.

We have examined five biblical values: love, fairness, mercy, respect and self-control. There are other areas that young people need help in developing. You can examine these on your own using the Test of Truth and the Evidence of Truth.

CHAPTER 14

Making It Right

Brittney Marsh closed the door as she left school. As she turned around, she almost ran into Matt.

"You frightened me!" she said.

Matt looked serious. "Can we talk?"

She agreed and began walking slowly toward home. Matt walked beside her.

"I still do not understand why you broke up with me," he said.

"I told you. I do not want to--" She looked around carefully. "I do not want to do those things anymore."

"But why not?" A bit of anger came into his voice. "I thought we were in love."

She stopped. "I thought so, too."

"So, I do not see what the problem is. I love you, Brittney. I just want to show you how much I love you."

She turned to look at him, "Can you show your love for me by waiting?"

"What do you mean?"

"Can you show how much you love me by waiting to have sex until we are married?"

"What are you talking about? You are fifteen! You cannot get married for – for years!"

Brittney was watching him but said nothing.

"You cannot be serious!" He searched her eyes. She did not look away. "Is it about that pregnancy thing?"

She raised a hand to silence him. He lowered his voice. "Is that what this is all about? I was just frightened, that is all. I would have been right there for you."

She turned and began walking again. Matt stepped in front of her and stopped, forcing her to stop. "Look, Brittney," he said. His voice was softer now. "I love you. I miss you." He placed his hands on her arms and kissed her neck.

She closed her eyes. He put one hand on her hair and kissed her again. "I want us to be together, like we were," he said gently. "I love you, Brittney, what is wrong with that?"

She opened her eyes and stepped back. "It is wrong," she said. Her dark eyes shone with understanding. "It is wrong because our kind of love was not willing to wait. Our love was not pure. Love should be a certain way, Matt. What we have been doing is not the way it should be."

"Why?"

"I was hiding things from my parents. That is what our 'love' made me do. I do not believe in that kind of thing anymore. When I had to take that pregnancy test, I was afraid. I was afraid of being pregnant. I was also afraid you might not stay around to take care of me. That is not the kind of love I am looking for."

"We can change all that. We can –

148

"No," she said. "It would still be wrong. I have had a mistaken idea about what makes something right or wrong. But I have been learning that my problem has been that I was trying to understand those things myself instead of looking to God for direction."

"God? What has God got to do with this?"

"He has everything to do with it. I cannot explain it as well as my mother can. But I know that something is right if it is like God. If it is not like God, it is wrong, and that means it is not going to make me happy. I am not going to have sex with anyone unless it includes a love that is pure and faithful to me for a lifetime in marriage. That is how it should be, Matt."

Matt looked hard at her. He could not believe what she was saying. "I do not know where you are getting all this, Brittney. Are you really going to let another person decide what is right for you?"

"Yes, I am. Because He knows much more than either of us do."

Those Who Move Old Landmarks

Brittney is beginning to put the truth to work in her life. She is learning to share the truth with others in her world. She may not always say the right thing. She may not be able to express herself exactly the way she wants to. But she is starting to take a stand for truth in a world that does not know much about truth. She is beginning to understand the value of limits in a world that is always trying to extend those limits.

The Prophet Hosea announced God's judgment against Judah's leaders. "The leaders of Judah are like those who take away the landmarks. I will pour out My anger on them like water" (Hosea 5:10). There are many people today who would move the old landmarks. They want to move the line between what is good and what is evil, what is right and what is wrong.

What used to be called sexual sin is now called one's sexual choice. What people once called shameful is now called art. A culture that once understood that God is the Judge of good and evil now looks to men to judge right from wrong.

But we are not powerless to oppose evil in the culture and begin to change it. After all, truth is on our side. We can pass on biblical values to our children even in a sin-loving and sin-sick world. We can take a stand against the insanity of a culture that is in rebellion against God. There are steps we can take to make it right in our homes, in our churches and in our neighborhoods.

Make It Right in Your Home

James Milford, Geena Santoro and Penny Marsh have begun to explore ways to make it right in their homes. They have begun building better relationships. They have begun teaching the Test of Truth and the Evidence of Truth to their children. They have begun to try to lead their children to the Person of Truth, Jesus Christ Himself.

If you want to make it right in your home, you must begin with yourself. Ask the Holy Spirit to show you in what ways you have moved away from the faith. Geena Santoro had to change her ideas of marriage. James Milford had to deal with the conflict between his teaching and his life. Penny Marsh had to understand that she had not been using truth in the same way in different situations. Do you want to make it right in your home? Ask the Holy Spirit to show you anything that would keep you from preparing your children to make the right choices.

Learn the Test of Truth and the Evidence of Truth. Use them to study the rules of God. Study what the Bible means when it commands us to "fear God." Study this book often. Study it with friends. Study other material that will help you master these truths. Work to make the Test of Truth and the Evidence of Truth so much a part of your thinking that it becomes second nature to you.

Teach these truths to your children. Before sharing the truths with your children, write out your goals for each of your children. I have discovered that if I write something down on paper, it becomes much clearer to me. Then I will understand it better and will work harder to do it.

Keep a written record of your thoughts. Talk about them when you sit at home and when you walk along the road, when you lie down and when you get up (Deuteronomy 6:7). Share with your family often what you believe about truth and right living.

Add to these the things found in chapter 8 on "Teaching the Truth." Strengthen your relationship with your children and others you want to influence. Be an example they can copy. Share the truth with them. "Be willing to wait for people to understand what you teach as you teach them" (2 Timothy 4:2). Lead those under your influence to the Person of Truth, Jesus Christ.

Make It Right in Your Church

James Milford is an example of what can happen when members of the Body of Christ begin holding each other accountable for sharing the truth in their families.

Parents, get this book into the hands of your pastor and youth worker. Pastors and youth workers, get this book into the hands of other church workers. Urge the people of your church to begin working together to learn right from wrong.

Pastors, use this book in your sermon planning. Make a series of messages that will use the material in this book. Prepare God's people to oppose evil in the culture. Plan times of prayer to fight against the sin in our homes and in our churches. Ask other churches to join in the effort.

Make It Right in Your Neighborhood

Much of this book has been about ways to teach biblical truth and ideas of right living in our families and in our churches. That is where we must begin. However, we must also be prepared to make it right in our neighborhoods.

If the culture has turned bad, it may be because the salt has not been doing its job! Jesus calls us to be salt. He calls us to fight against the ideas that would ruin our society. We cannot expect a dark world to light itself. We must be the light (see Matthew 5:13-15). We have wondered why our culture has become so bad while many Christians have failed to be the salt and light God meant for them to be.

We cannot hide from our world. Our young people will face questions and arguments from teachers, from the media and from their friends and neighbors. We must teach them how to oppose evil in the culture in our own neighborhoods. We also must show them how to do it.

How to Oppose Evil in the Culture

In April 1980, a group of U.S. soldiers was sent on a secret mission to rescue a group of Americans in Iran. The Americans had been held hostage there for about six months. The soldiers were highly trained. Their equipment was the best the nation had. The plan was carefully made. The mission ended in failure, though. There were many problems with the equipment. A great cloud of dust made it hard to see. As a result eight of the soldiers died and the Americans were still held hostage.

Many good ideas have failed. If we are to help renew a sense of right and wrong in our neighborhoods, we must listen to Jesus' warning to be "wise like snakes and gentle like doves" (Matthew 10:16). We must plan, prepare and work with wisdom and careful thinking.

Here are five things you can do.

1. Choose your issues wisely. Many sinful things are happening in our neighborhoods. But we cannot speak out on every issue. We would soon be too tired to do anything. We would probably also become known as troublemakers. If we want to be effective, we should begin by choosing one issue that is clearly against what most people believe is right.

People are beginning to see the insanity all around us. Newspapers report it. The most unlikely voices are being raised to protest the things that are threatening our culture, our families and our children.

You and I can step in with an answer that can protect our neighborhoods and our children from the pain of a world gone insane. We can provide an answer that takes us back to the true ideas of right and wrong. But we must be careful to choose our issues wisely, especially in the beginning.

2. Get others to join with you. There is influence in numbers. Talk to others in your church, school system and neighborhood. Choose an issue that everyone agrees should be opposed.

3. Know why the thing is wrong. The Bible says, "Always be ready to tell everyone who asks you why you believe as you do. Be gentle as you speak and show respect" (1 Peter 3:15).

Be prepared to explain and defend what you believe. Appeal to people's sense of what is right and best for their children. People react better when they believe someone has their children's best interest at heart. They stop listening, though, when they think someone is trying to "save lost souls."

This does not mean that people should not begin to understand that your ideas are based on the nature of God. It means that we should obey the biblical advice to "speak with them in such a way they will want to listen to you. Do not let your talk sound foolish. Know how to give the right answer to anyone" (Colossians 4:6).

4. Be prepared to be opposed. As soon as we use the Bible to defend our ideas we will be called intolerant. "That is the problem with you people," we will be told. "It is either your way or no way. You have no right to force your beliefs on other people."

Tolerance has become the only good that western culture values. Intolerance is the only evil that western culture sees as wrong. Tolerance is praised as the new way of judging between right and wrong. Chuck Colson put the problem this way in his book *The Body*:

> . . . the only good left in the modern world is unlimited tolerance. The modern mind says that all values are equally good if the person really believes them. But that does not include the value of faithfulness to absolute truth. To the modern mind, there are no absolutes except the absolute that there can be no absolutes.

Public schools can teach that two men can live together as husband and wife. If a parent opposes such teaching, he is called "intolerant." A person can show pictures of naked people in public and call it art. If a Christian opposes it, she is called "intolerant." Anyone who opposes sin in public places is accused of opposing the personal rights of others.

It is not a good thing to tolerate things that threaten the right living or safety of our children. The Bible makes it clear that "the fear of the Lord is to hate what is sinful" (Proverbs 8:13). We may anger those who do not want to live by what is right. But Jesus warned us, "If the world hates you, you know it hated Me before it hated you" (John 15:18). We must not seek opposition, but we should not be surprised when it comes.

5. *Oppose ideas, not people*. The Apostle Peter warned Christians to always be "ready to tell everyone who asks you why you believe as you do" (I Peter 3:15). Just before that he commanded us to "share the same thoughts and the same feelings. Love each other with a kind heart and with a mind that has no pride. When someone does something bad to you, do not do the same thing

154

to him. When someone talks about you, do not talk about him. Instead, pray that good will come to him" (1 Peter 3:8-9).

A little later Peter advised, "Keep your heart telling you that you have done what is right. If men speak against you, they will be ashamed when they see the good way you have lived as a Christian" (1 Peter 3:16).

Remember that men are not arguing with us. They are arguing with the truth. It is not us they reject. It is the Truth, Jesus Himself. If we remember that, we will understand that the enemies of truth should not be the objects of our hate. We should love them because God loves them (see John 3:16, Romans 5:8 and 2 Peter 3:9).

It is possible "to make it right" in our homes and in our churches. We can even begin making it right in our neighborhoods. We can renew "the fear of God" in ourselves and in our families and churches. We can prepare ourselves and our children with the Test of Truth and the Evidence of Truth. We can take a stand for truth in our neighborhoods. Once we are prepared, we are ready to make it right and to "be able to stand in that sinful day" (Ephesians 6:13).

Note About International English

Special International is a group of about 1,500 root or basic English words. A different beginning (prefix) and ending (suffix) may be added to these words to change or add to the meaning. For example, when the prefix "un" is added to the word "happy" it becomes "unhappy," meaning "not happy." When the suffix "ly" is added to the word "God" it becomes "godly," meaning "God like." When these are learned, many more words are easy to understand. Below is a list of many prefixes and suffixes with their meanings that are used in this book.

Prefixes:

dis-:	apart, away, not *[disappear, dislike]*
in-:	**1.** in, into *[inside]* **2.** not *[indirect]*
pre-:	before *[preheat]*
re-:	**1.** back *[repay]* **2.** again *[retell]*
un-:	not *[untie]*

Suffixes:

-able:	able to *[readable]*
-ed:	**1.** past tense (happened before) *[added]*
	2. having *[watered]*
-en:	**1.** to become, *[weaken]*
	2. made of, *[wooden]*
	3. completed action, *[written]*
-ence or	
-ance:	in a condition, or act of, *[silence]*
-er:	**1.** one who, *[reader]*
	2. comparing, *[harder]*
-est:	more than all others, *[hardest, softest]*
-ful:	**1.** full of, like, *[thankful]*
-ing:	the act of, [praying]; produced by the action of, *[drawing]*; or something that does the action of, *[covering]*

-ion or

-tion: the condition of or result of, *[connection]*

-ive: belonging to or tending to, *[effective, active]*

-less: without *[godless]*

-ly: like *[godly]*

-ment: the condition or act of, *[agreement]*

-ness: condition of being, *[greatness]*

-s, es: plural (more than one), *[Bibles]*